putting the humanities PhD to work

Putting the Humanities PhD to Work

thriving in and beyond the classroom

Katina L. Rogers

DUKE UNIVERSITY PRESS   DURHAM AND LONDON   2020

© 2020 Duke University Press
All rights reserved
Printed in the United States of America on acid-free paper ∞
Designed by Drew Sisk
Typeset in Portrait Text Regular by Copperline Book Services

Library of Congress Cataloging-in-Publication Data
Names: Rogers, Katina L., author.
Title: Putting the humanities PhD to work : thriving in
and beyond the classroom / Katina L. Rogers.
Description: Durham : Duke University Press, 2020. |
Includes bibliographical references and index.
Identifiers: LCCN 2019047830 (print) |
LCCN 2019047831 (ebook)
ISBN 9781478008613 (hardcover)
ISBN 9781478009542 (paperback)
ISBN 9781478012207 (ebook)
Subjects: LCSH: College graduates—Employment—United
States. | Graduate students—Employment—United States. |
Doctor of philosophy degree—United States. | Humanities—
Study and teaching (Graduate)—United States.
Classification: LCC HD6278.U5 R64 2020 (print) |
LCC HD6278.U5 (ebook) | DDC 331.11/4450973—dc23
LC record available at https://lccn.loc.gov/2019047830
LC ebook record available at https://lccn.loc.gov/2019047831

Cover art: Illustration and design by Drew Sisk

Duke University Press gratefully acknowledges the Professional
Staff Congress at CUNY, which provided funds toward the
publication of this book.

CONTENTS

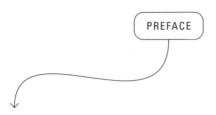

In writing this book, I have drawn on my research on career pathways and graduate education reform as well as personal experience. My academic and professional route has taken me from a PhD in comparative literature, through education-focused positions at foundations and nonprofits, to my current position at the Graduate Center, City University of New York, where I serve as codirector for the Futures Initiative and director of programs and administration for the Humanities, Arts, Science, and Technology Alliance and Collaboratory (HASTAC). That pathway serves as a personal case study for the key tenet of this book: that even in this challenging time for higher education, a PhD in the humanities is worth pursuing for the training it offers, the doors it opens, and the value it provides to society. Informed by extensive research, interviews, and practical advice from dozens of sources, *Putting the Humanities PhD to Work* provides graduate students, faculty members, and administrators concrete examples of how this kind of pathway is possible, how it can be pursued, and where it can lead.

The message I offer in this book differs from the one I first received when I began my own graduate career. In my first year as a graduate student in comparative literature, I learned that the humanities were in crisis. More precisely, I was told that the humanities both *were presently* and *had always been* in crisis—that in an abstract sense, and quite apart from the very real problems in academic labor structures, crisis was one of the fundamental ways the field understood and continually redefined itself. As the first in my immediate family to pursue a PhD, I absorbed that message from my first-year seminar course without being dissuaded by it. In retrospect, I often think about the ways that framing could have derailed what has since become a meaningful and rewarding career. After nearly twenty years working in and around graduate education, I have had countless occasions to see the ways that the lens of perpetual crisis is both lamented and, in some ways, revered in the humanities. I am glad to be able to circle back and think more critically about the pervasiveness and problematic nature of that framing—not only in my program, but in much of the writing about humanities research and doctoral study. One motivation in writing this book is to provide balanced research and practical advice both to those who, like me, come to graduate education without the social grounding to contextualize these issues, as well as to those who already have a framework for understanding the challenges of academe and want to go deeper.

I have made decisions about my own career path based on a complex set of needs, desires, circumstances, and experience, as everyone does. I completed my own PhD in 2010 in Comparative Literature at the University of Colorado, Boulder. "Quit Lit" wasn't yet a thing, or if it was, I didn't know about it. I had never heard of "alt-ac," the playful neologism coined a year prior in a Twitter conversation between Jason Rhody, digital culture program director at the Social Science Research Council, and Bethany Nowviskie, Dean of Libraries and Professor of English at James Madison University, as they tried to find the best way to characterize their own unusual, hybrid, not-faculty-but-still-scholarly jobs. As Nowviskie puts it, the use of the term was a means of "gesturing at an alternative academia" in the way that writers create speculative fiction or works of alternative history.[1] "Alt" as a modifier was also reminiscent of the early days of the internet, hearkening back to the hierarchies of Usenet forums, and perhaps struck a chord with the digital humanities community for that reason.[2] It was a lighthearted term, never meant to be used in an authoritative way, and yet it stuck around as employment patterns continued to change in and around the academy.

Within this world of hybrid scholarly careers, specific roles are varied and unique, which can make it challenging to know what kinds of opportunities are available. This has certainly been true for me; there was no clear pathway set before me. At each decision point in my career, I found it difficult to predict where I might be a few years later, and where a particular decision might lead. I share my story here as a single example of one possible trajectory—one that I personally have found exciting and satisfying. Though the details differ, there are many, many stories like mine. The work I have been able to do along this path has offered unexpected opportunities to think systematically about higher education, and to be a part of conversations and projects that have real impact beyond my own discipline. As a graduate student, I could not have anticipated that I would one day work on major, multi-institutional grants connecting graduate education and community college teaching, or that I would field questions from journalists at the *New York Times* and the *Chronicle of Higher*

Education about the implications of my work, or that I would have opportunities to review projects and proposals far outside my disciplinary background.

The job that I consider to be the first significant step in my career initially came about as a means of hedging my bets. I had moved cross-country while working on my dissertation, so I no longer had institutional funding and needed an income while I continued to research and write. I started working with a temp agency whose clients were primarily foundations and nonprofits. The work was not very interesting in itself, at least at first; I sought temp work because I thought it would leave me enough brain space at the end of the day and on weekends to do research, and it did. But over time, learning about the inner workings of grantmaking organizations began to fascinate me. A few of my short-term jobs were with the Alfred P. Sloan Foundation, which funds research in science and technology. I established strong relationships with a number of the foundation's staff members, and when a full-time position opened, they invited me to apply.

As I see it, this first opportunity worked out for a number of reasons: for one thing, Sloan is an institution that places a high value on scholarship. Though I was trained in a different field than most of my science-minded colleagues, they respected the discipline and deep curiosity that graduate study entails. In addition, my résumé showed that I was an effective translator, both in terms of language and also, more figuratively, in terms of articulating ideas across different groups of people or disciplines. As a graduate student, I had worked part-time at another science organization, the International Union of Geodesy and Geophysics, where I had been hired for my fluency in French, one of the organization's official languages. I certainly didn't expect that job to have anything to do with my future career path, but looking back, I'm convinced it made me a more appealing candidate at Sloan. A final and important factor in securing the role at Sloan was that I had a foot in the door through the temp jobs. The staff had had a chance to get to know me and my work in a way they wouldn't have been able to know through simply an application and an interview.

While at Sloan, my responsibilities steadily increased, and by the end of my employment I was actively contributing to the strategic development of an entirely new program area, called digital information technology, under the direction of Joshua M. Greenberg. Though rooted in science, technology, engineering, and math (STEM) fields, the new program had much in common with the digital humanities and the changing terrain of scholarly communication across all academic disciplines. I contributed to the strategic planning process of identifying pressing questions, leading thinkers, and opportunities for meaningful grantmaking. At the same time, I was gaining invaluable understanding about the grant evaluation process, as well as the nuts and bolts of organizational structures and operations—things I certainly hadn't learned as a graduate student.

Another thing that my work at Sloan taught me was that some of the most interesting conversations about higher education were happening in open online environments, like Twitter. This is old news now, but it was new to me at the time. As I began looking for new opportunities for growth, I made a pointed effort to develop a more visible professional online presence than I had previously done. I connected with people on Twitter, blogged about issues in higher education, and listened in to online conversations to get a feel for who was doing the kind of work I wanted to do and what kinds of positions might interest me. This was how I eventually connected with Bethany Nowviskie, who later hired me as a researcher with the Scholarly Communication Institute (SCI), which was then based in the University of Virginia Libraries. The institute is a Mellon-funded humanities think tank that, at the time I was hired, had dedicated ten years to investigating the changing environment of scholarly communication and graduate education. Without the work I had done at Sloan and my exploration of Twitter and blogging, I doubt that I even would have caught wind of the work that SCI was doing. I was also fortunate in that Sloan carries a significant amount of prestige in academic circles, which made it easier for me to make connections and earn credibility.

When I began my position at SCI, new challenges awaited me. Part of my job was to design and administer a survey of people with advanced humanities degrees who had pursued career paths beyond the tenure track. But I had no prior background in survey methodology or analysis, and so I knew I would have to learn and apply a complex set of new skills quickly, albeit with a great deal of support and insight from the university's research librarians.[3] To have opportunities for continued growth was deeply exciting, and I think that in my case, such opportunities have been possible precisely because I have applied my deep academic training to a nonfaculty job.

My work at SCI led to new networking opportunities, deeper experience in the changing world of graduate education, and a clearer sense of how important the nuances of scholarly communication systems (publishers, libraries, formal and informal online platforms, and so on—all the ways scholars share their research) are to the entire academic enterprise. When my eighteen-month employment term at SCI had run its course, I began working at the Modern Language Association (MLA) under Kathleen Fitzpatrick, then the director of scholarly communication, whom I had met while at Sloan and worked with at SCI. At the MLA, I worked with Fitzpatrick and other colleagues to think through similar questions of how researchers share their work in an online networked environment on a broader scale, with nationwide and international impact. While the role was very different from any of my previous positions, it was while working at the MLA that, for the first time, I sensed a certain cohesiveness in the direction that my career was taking.

As I write this, I am in my sixth year with the Futures Initiative, a program located within the Graduate Center of the City University of New York (CUNY). At the Futures Initiative, my colleagues and I work toward institutional change in higher education through a dual focus on equity and innovation. I hadn't expected my path to lead back to the university, but I'm delighted that it has. While I don't regularly teach in a classroom, as codirector I find myself applying so many skills, methods, and insights that I gained during my graduate studies—as well as many that I have learned experientially. Together with Cathy N. Davidson, the Futures Initiative's founding director and a steadfast mentor, I work on our program's strategy, mission, and programming; write and implement grants; guide and mentor our team of graduate fellows; manage our program's budgets; and more, all while continuing to research and write. It has been an exciting and exhilarating place to work. With over 500,000 students, CUNY is the largest public, urban university system in the United States, and it is deeply woven into the fabric of New York City. [4] Working with students, faculty, and administrators here has opened my eyes to a wide range of stories and experiences, centering on the power of education and the importance of access to it. Understanding education as a public good in the context of a huge public university system in the heart of a thriving city that is also home to massive income inequality means that engaging with a broader community is critical to what we do. I am constantly learning, and I have the distinct joy of knowing that our work matters.

Getting to this point has had many challenges, but there are also many ways that my path has been smoothed both by privilege and by luck. I worked with an advisor who supported and respected my decisions and who didn't pressure me to pursue a particular type of career. My partner has stable employment, which reduced the anxiety of my own job search and kept me in health insurance through temporary jobs and times of uncertainty. Along the way, some opportunities turned out to be more important than I anticipated, and served as unexpected stepping-stones in new directions. Plus, importantly, as a straight white woman, I do not typically face bias for my race, ethnicity, or sexuality, and so I move through the world with significant privilege. I detail these attributes of my own academic career and personal experience to signal a range of factors that most discussions of the state of the humanities do not address as part of the larger narrative.

While all of these elements have served to minimize the obstacles I encountered, I have also worked hard to make my own luck, as Sarah Werner, an independent book history and Shakespeare scholar forging her own unique career path, has described.[5] I share those experiences, too, for the way they can help others in their own career trajectories. During my years as a graduate student, I accumulated job experience that seemed practical but inconsequential until I learned how to translate my skills into a more meaningful narrative. As I approached the end of my dissertation, I was intentional about developing a semiprofessional online presence and meeting people who were doing work that I found interesting and valuable. My research had always been a little bit "meta" and became increasingly so, as slowly my focus shifted from trauma and formal experimentation in twentieth- and twenty-first century French literature to the structures of graduate education itself, with my own career path as a case study in my research. All of these actions helped me to build a strong foundation and to be ready for opportunities when they arose.

Some graduate students worry about the risk of seeming overqualified for positions that don't necessarily require a PhD. What I have found is that the doctoral degree opens up entire pathways, rather than a single job opportunity. The first step in that trajectory may not require the amount of specialized knowledge that doctoral recipients have amassed, but new opportunities for advancement and increased responsibilities often open up quickly. Early on, I did find that the PhD was a slippery credential; in some professional settings it wasn't relevant at all (like reviewing and processing compliance materials for financial and health benefits at Sloan); in others, it led people to trust me to take on difficult tasks even though they were outside my area of expertise (like strategic development at Sloan, survey work at SCI, and leadership and management at CUNY). In almost all cases, though, holding a graduate degree meant that I enjoyed a greater amount of credibility, especially among current and former faculty members or others deeply involved in higher education. A PhD in any field is a strong indicator of dedication, hard work, intellectual stamina, judgment, and an ability to learn quickly and deeply; when that degree is in a humanities field, it also signals exceptional skills in areas such as critical thinking, interpretation, cultural understanding, and communication—especially writing, which is highly valued in nearly every workplace.

Developing new skills has been an important part of my trajectory, and learning the basics of web development, data visualization, and survey analysis has been crucial to my work. Rapid advances in digital capabilities and deeper connections across the humanities and computational fields—both computational humanities and the critical study and creation of new media—have led to new insight, closer interdisciplinary collaboration, and opportunities for broad impact beyond the university. Learning HTML and CSS, understanding the power of the command line, and beginning to know which kinds of technical problems are easy to solve and which ones are harder all make it easier for humanities scholars to work alongside people from other disciplines and join in projects that push toward new knowledge. But skills like these tend to be most valuable when they are mandated by a particular project, rather than explored as ends in themselves. Pushing all humanities students to learn to code isn't a quick fix to systemic labor issues; however, making it possible for students to pursue the kinds of projects that spark genuine interest, and making it possible for them to learn necessary skills along the way, will likely lead to more creative and interesting research projects while also building up digital literacy and skills that may be transferable to other job contexts.

I hope this book might help others to find their footing on their own individual paths, wherever those may lead. For me, several key factors throughout my trajectory have been to seek and learn from mentors, to open myself up to people and opportunities, to recognize and stay attuned to my changing interests, to communicate widely through different media platforms, and to take steps that seem promising even if I don't know where they'll lead. I've always tried to maintain a sense of growth and progress that help ensure that I'm a competitive candidate for new kinds of roles. The flexibility of my path is, for me, one of its most appealing qualities; I feel a stronger sense of agency in crafting my career than I might have if I had followed a more "traditional" path. It is time—past time—to rethink the expectations that many students and faculty bring to graduate study and its outcomes, especially those that effectively limit students' future potential and the reach of their work. It is time for a broader understanding of what constitutes scholarly excellence.

This book is not only about individual success, but also institutional change. Now more than ever, vocal support for the value of the humanities is essential. The current US political climate leaves our national arts and humanities organizations woefully underfunded and a pen stroke away from total elimination. The problems facing the academy as a whole are real, and serious: the rampant defunding of public higher education, where 80 percent of US students attend college; the disastrous effects on academic labor structures and hiring; the huge amounts of debt that students accrue; the persistent bias against women and nonbinary people of all races and ethnicities, and people of color of all genders. I acknowledge these problems while also celebrating the positive signs that change might be coming and finding ways to work toward institutional change. Conversations about career pathways, labor structures, and diversity and inclusion all have interrelated dependencies, and trying to isolate a single issue without addressing the others leads to partial solutions at best. Instead, bringing about meaningful and lasting reform means finding a way to both recognize the realities of the current landscape and also push for change in many directions at once.

For me, this work is personal as well as intellectual, a reflection of the pathway and research I have pursued. The connection reminds me constantly that intellectual pursuits are never separate from the many other elements of a person's life and experience. I bring that recognition to the book, with the hope that readers at many stages of their life paths and career paths will find it to be a balanced and useful framework for their own personal, intellectual, and professional circumstances.

ACKNOWLEDGMENTS

The existence of this book—my first—feels exhilarating and impossible. The research and writing process has coincided with my husband Ajay and I becoming parents, twice over. The book feels deeply tied to that transformation, to the changes in perspectives that parenthood has brought, and to Ajay's support throughout it all. I dedicate the book to our two kids, Anika and Siva, and to the many possible futures that await them.

Along the same lines, I want to acknowledge that the book could not possibly exist without the support of our kids' caregivers and teachers. To the many daycare providers, teachers, and other caregivers who have supported our family along the way: thank you. My heart overflows with gratitude.

This book has been immeasurably improved by the wisdom and insight of Maureen McCarthy, Stacy Hartman, and Jade Davis, all of whom were generous, encouraging, and critical readers who helped me to trust that this book could really become something while also helping me to see ways to strengthen it. I was also fortunate to discuss ideas and share early drafts with many friends and colleagues, including Erin Fletcher, Kathleen Fitzpatrick, Monica McCormick, Shana Kimball, Amanda Watson, Patricia Hswe, Syelle Graves, and countless internet friends. I'm also grateful to have had the opportunity to speak with many colleagues at conferences, talks, and workshops over the past few years, where thoughtful discussions and questions have sharpened my thinking. Thank you all so much for providing a sounding board for my ideas and helping me to find and trust my voice.

Danica Savonick worked with me as a research assistant at a key point in the book's development, and her invaluable feedback helped all the pieces come together. I am grateful for her many excellent suggestions and her help in moving through a plateau and bringing the book closer to completion. Likewise, I am indebted to the support of Cihan Tekay, who worked with me as a research assistant in the later stages of the book's editing and production. Her professionalism, sharp eye, and thoughtfulness were invaluable in the final stages, and she also helped bring the book's ideas to life through a national conference at the Graduate Center. Thank you both!

My thinking has been shaped by amazing and generous mentors along the way: Bethany Nowviskie and Abby Smith Rumsey, who made the original data collection possible and showed me new ways of thinking; Josh Greenberg, who introduced me to many new people and ideas and encouraged me to explore new intellectual terrain; Cathy N. Davidson, whose vision and support have opened up new horizons; and Warren Motte and Patricia Paige at the University of Colorado, both of whom helped me think expansively about my own future pathway. I have long been inspired by Kelley Barsanti and Jo Ann Joselyn, brilliant women with astonishing careers in science whom I am lucky to have as members of my extended family. I am deeply grateful to my parents for their unwavering support and encouragement.

This book would not be what it is without my incredible colleagues at CUNY, as well as at the Modern Language Association and the University of Virginia. I feel so fortunate to work with such thoughtful, creative people who are willing to engage deeply with one another's ideas, and working in such a wide range of roles—including graduate students, undergraduate students, faculty, administrators, postdoctoral fellows, librarians, data scientists, and more.

The project has been materially supported by two research grants from my union, the Professional Staff Congress, PSC-CUNY. Earlier stages of work were made possible by the Andrew W. Mellon Foundation's support of the Scholarly Communication Institute. I am so appreciative of the institutional support.

Finally, there would be no book without Ken Wissoker, who saw a spark of something that could be bigger; the team at Duke University Press; and the generosity and insight of three incredible readers who pushed the book to be the best it could be. Thank you all for making this possible.

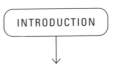

Putting the PhD to Work— for the Public Good

This book invites readers to consider ways that humanities graduate training can open unexpected doors that lead to meaningful careers with significant public impact, while also suggesting that an expanded understanding of scholarly success can foster more equitable and inclusive systems in and around the academy. It offers concrete steps to support individual career pathways as well as structural reform. Despite decades of research and funding in career initiatives, many doctoral students feel alone and at sea when it comes to envisioning and working toward their professional futures. And yet an increasingly interconnected world means that the humanities are more necessary than ever. It is because of this disconnect—between students' frustrations on one hand, and the importance of the humanities in all sectors on the other—that I began this project. Intended especially for doctoral students and their faculty mentors and advisors, *Putting the Humanities PhD to Work* includes case studies and concrete actions to broaden the range of career paths for those who pursue doctoral education. And yet it is more than a how-to guide. The underlying pulse of the book continually returns to two main questions:

→ What can be done—by students, faculty, and program administrators—to normalize and strengthen a wider range of career pathways?

→ How might a broader understanding of postgraduate success improve the health and inclusivity of the humanities?

These questions help to situate a discussion of career paths in a broader context of graduate education reform and support for higher education as a public good. Graduate education is sometimes perceived as elite and esoteric, but scholarly research has a significant impact on things that affect the daily lives of millions—from the policies that structure our society to the stories and art that bring meaning and joy. This book offers ways to reframe humanities doctoral training with an eye toward public impact, and a focus on making graduate education matter in new and powerful ways.

I contend that reform can and should take place at multiple levels simultaneously, with students, faculty, and administrators all creating opportunities for change through decisions large and small. The book is intended for current, prospective, and recent graduate students; for scholars who are interested in changing careers at any life stage; and for faculty members, graduate deans, administrators, and advisors who shape graduate programs as well as individual students' pathways. Each of these audiences may have a different goal in reading this book—embarking on a different career path, learning new strategies for advising students, understanding the current landscape of graduate education before deciding whether to pursue a PhD. By providing a solid background of the stakes and possible interventions, as well as practical, hands-on advice, I hope every reader emerges with a clear sense of possibility for their particular context as well as a glimpse into the hopes, values, concerns, and constraints facing other readers.

This book includes a consideration of academic labor structures and career opportunities, and provides graduate students with a context and analytical framework for discerning opportunities for different potential career paths, while taking an activist perspective that moves not only toward individual success but also toward systemic change. For those in positions to make decisions in humanities departments or programs, the book offers insight into the circumstances and pressures that students are facing and examples of programmatic reform that address career matters in structural ways. It grounds its argument in recent data without losing sight of the human realities that suffuse issues of academic labor practices, job markets, and career paths. Throughout, I highlight the important truth that different kinds of careers might offer engaging, fulfilling, and even unexpected pathways for students who seek them out. People pursuing PhDs are deeply curious, exploratory, and passionate about their work; that curiosity is essential to research. Imagine what could happen if doctoral students were invited to apply a similar approach of inquiry, creativity, and exploration to their potential professional lives beyond the university's gates.

Individuals and institutions can play a pivotal role in supporting a renewal of humanities education as a key element of thoughtful citizenship in today's society. My research suggests that new developments in doctoral programs—like encouraging creative dissertation formats, adopting new models for comprehensive exams, integrating digital skills and methods into humanities scholarship, and embracing scholarship with meaningful public impact—can open doors to broader matters of where students work and how scholarship might reach the public in unexpected ways. Solid mentorship is also key, as it gives students the space to explore their possible futures, equip them for broader pathways, and enliven their research. From small interventions to major programmatic change, there are ways for students, faculty, and administrators to begin working toward these goals right now.

Recognizing the expansive social value of the knowledge, skills, and approaches that recent graduates have gained during the course of their studies means understanding the wide range of institutions and contexts where they can make a significant impact. Faculty and administrators have an opportunity to adjust graduate program structures to better equip students to take on a wide range of roles where they can apply their deep humanities training. Even without knowing exactly what pathway a graduate might take, since career opportunities are constantly evolving, the curiosity and love of learning that spark a desire to pursue a graduate degree is something to celebrate. Society needs more, not fewer, people trained to understand and contextualize the cultural, historical, linguistic, and other valences of contemporary geopolitics. More people who can read, critique, and synthesize complex and competing arguments. More people who know the national and global histories of systemic racism and institutionalized bias and who are equipped to speak out against ongoing inequalities. We need them in the classroom—but not only there. The impact of humanities training would be far greater if universities trained students not only to teach but also enabled them to pursue careers that carried them beyond the university, creating a robust network of humanities PhDs working across a wide range of institutions and professional contexts.

In fact, the nodes for such a network do exist, since humanities PhDs have long excelled in a wide range of careers. Doctoral degree recipients have very low rates of unemployment, and those working beyond the classroom, whether in nonprofits or businesses, tend to have very high rates of job satisfaction—higher than those in tenure-track faculty positions.[1] Research by the Modern Language Association suggests that the trend of strong employment for people with advanced degrees holds true for the humanities, with only 0.1 percent unemployment in their sample.[2] However, this network of PhDs working beyond the classroom remains somewhat invisible in university contexts. It is not uncommon for department websites to unceremoniously drop the names of their graduates who step into jobs outside the familiar ranks of assistant, associate, full—especially since only faculty job placements count toward program rankings. Alumni networks and development offices are the first to know when grads have made a move, but departments often rapidly lose touch. Rather than forming a vibrant network of the multivalent possibilities open to humanities PhDs, those who seek careers outside the classroom quietly disappear, leaving each new generation of students to wonder what they could possibly do with their degrees—and prompting countless would-be students to decide not even to apply. Since graduate students excel at reading between the lines, the silences speak loudly. When certain outcomes are celebrated and others are rendered invisible, there is a tacit but clear signal that paths outside the well-trodden ones are undesirable. The result is a perpetuation of conventional forms of success, which limits creativity and diversity of all kinds, and also limits any extramural connections that students might have fostered. Given the already-widespread perception that the humanities are less valuable than STEM fields in terms of applicability and practicality, advisors, departments, and universities are taking an enormous risk by sending such messages.

Imagine an example. Picture a student just beginning her graduate work in, say, English; I'll call her Eva. She dives into the coursework, learning the methodological and theoretical approaches that her discipline values. She plunges into close reading and archival research. She learns about the historical context, the contemporary stakes, and the counternarratives that affect her research. She selects an advisor and a committee to guide and critique her work. As she learns more and more about the ways that literature has given voice to important cultural moments, she is inspired by the possibility that connecting communities with art and literature in new and deeper ways may serve to bring about new insight, cross-cultural understanding, self-reflection, and a deeper grasp of historical context. Perhaps she looks ahead to her future career and pictures herself working with the public in an advocacy capacity, navigating between local work with a community-based organization and broader outreach through op-eds and public speaking. As she gains experience and credibility, she finds that she is able to bring her deep humanities training to bear on public perception and educational policy work.

But now imagine that as Eva shares her enthusiasm, she begins noticing implicit messages of disapproval from her professors and even fellow students.

She perceives flashes of confusion or displeasure about her proposed path. Her advisor is unable to suggest any models or mentors for her to turn to for guidance. She has a difficult time finding resources to help her make connections and explore opportunities. Faced with these negative signals, she decides to pursue the expected path and go on the academic job market.

Though Eva's research is excellent, tenure-line faculty positions make up an ever-smaller share of college instructional positions, while doctoral graduation rates continue to increase. Undergraduate enrollments are strong despite a decrease in the number of humanities majors, and colleges need someone to teach all those students, so this newly minted PhD is able to pick up a few courses as an adjunct. Suddenly finding herself earning less money than she did as a graduate student, she cobbles together odd jobs to keep herself afloat. With no time built into her job description for research or professional development that would make her a more competitive candidate for tenure-track positions, it becomes increasingly difficult for her to break out of the cycle.

Now imagine that Eva is forward-looking and perceives all of these possible outcomes before she begins her graduate career. Perhaps she is the first in her family to attend college. Perhaps she is a woman of color, and notices very quickly that there are few people who look like her among the ranks of senior faculty across the United States, giving her the impression that the profession will be unwelcoming or that she will face bias throughout her trajectory. Given all those factors, does she decide to take five or ten years out of the workforce, relocate, and possibly go into debt in order to pursue a graduate degree? She may decide that the odds are not in her favor and opt out before she even begins.

While Eva considers these possible outcomes, the department she is (or was) considering conducts a calculus of its own. Faculty and administrators observe that their graduates are having a difficult time gaining long-term academic positions, and in response the department grows increasingly conservative in its admissions process. Rather than take risks on students with unconventional backgrounds or those who hope to do the kind of public-focused work that Eva hoped to do, they redouble their efforts to recruit conventionally high-achieving prospective students with top-notch GRE scores and pristine academic pedigrees. In what they think is an unrelated issue, they are surprised to note as the years pass that they are having a harder and harder time meeting university goals for diversity and representation among their students, and even among their new faculty hires.

This scenario is all too common in higher education, and shows how many issues intertwine to create an environment that is problematic from both an educational and a social justice standpoint. It is a no-win situation. The individual student is badly served by the systemic biases, exploitative labor structures, and negative signals she receives from her peers and advisors. The department is negatively affected by the well-meaning but problematic move toward increased conservatism that they hope will improve placement rates for their graduates, but that actually serve to further reduce diversity and limit opportunity. Undergraduate students are badly served by the poor labor practices of most institutions that leave adjunct faculty teaching the most vulnerable undergraduate populations with extremely limited resources and support.

There's another major segment of the population that is badly served by this scenario: the public. Because Eva received signals that nudged her toward a career in the classroom that she wasn't initially aiming for and away from a fulfilling public-oriented career that appealed to her, the public is deprived of a deeply trained specialist who could help advocate for complex causes that require deft historical inquiry and cultural understanding.

The focus of this book is only partially about the success of individuals; it is also intrinsically tied to broader cultural norms and labor issues within the academy.[3] Though humanities scholars thrive in a wide range of positions (and have long done so), most doctoral students in the humanities consider a faculty position to be their primary career goal, and few graduate programs systematically equip their students for varied postgraduate opportunities. And yet meaningful and sustainable academic employment is an increasingly distant prospect for many doctoral recipients, with a dwindling proportion of tenure-track jobs available to an ever-growing pool of graduates. In 2016, 37.5 percent of all graduating humanities PhDs reported having an academic job lined up— and many of these positions were likely adjunct positions or short-term visiting appointments (I'll have more to say about that in chapter 1). Most do find work in the years following graduation—the overall unemployment rate for humanities PhDs is very low—but it can take people a few years to find their footing. Given these numbers, so-called "alternative" career options are anything but secondary.[4] A more expansive view of career possibilities might enable recent graduates to find meaningful work more quickly by encouraging a different kind of search from the outset.

Even though the percentage of graduates that obtain tenure-track faculty positions has diminished as reliance on contingent labor increases, faculty careers are still the primary goal for a large majority of humanities doctoral students. Findings from "Humanities Unbound," a study I conducted with the Scholarly Communications Institute in 2012, revealed that three out of four PhDs working *outside* the classroom entered graduate school expecting to pursue a career in the professoriate.[5] As the American Association of University

Professors notes in their annual report on the state of the profession, academic employment is increasingly shifting to part-time and contingent positions, with 76 percent of all teaching positions being filled by instructors in contingent roles as of 2011.[6] This trend means that proportionally fewer tenure-track lines are available to new graduates, compounding the problem. Notably, a 2013 survey of chief academic officers revealed that provosts expected that reliance on adjunct labor to continue or increase; some respondents expressed having little faith in a continued tenure system.[7] Given this backdrop, continuing to view tenure-track employment as the sole expected professional outcome for humanities doctoral recipients is untenable.

The fact that tenure-track employment opportunities are becoming scarcer relative to the number of graduates does not necessarily mean that too many people earn PhDs, or that graduate programs should reduce their admissions. The truth is that the high percentage of contingent faculty members has not come about due to an overabundance of doctoral recipients. Rather, the decision to have adjuncts teach the large majority of college courses is an almost entirely separate matter of budgetary pressure and institutional priorities that favor short-term and inexpensive solutions over long-term and complex commitments to departments, programs, and students. While some contingent positions offer reasonable wages and benefits, the vast majority do not. The matter goes beyond simple supply and demand; the number of tenure-track positions available does not fluctuate based on the number of qualified candidates, or even based on the number of students enrolling in a particular disciplinary area. Changing the supply of newly minted PhDs by offering more or fewer slots in graduate programs will likely have little to no effect on the job market for tenure-track faculty careers.

A number of institutions are working against these patterns, and throughout this book I share examples of those whose approaches are particularly compelling. From incremental changes like modifying the curriculum for a single course, to more sweeping reform that takes aim at things like dissertation models or time-to-degree across an institution, many programs are beginning (or continuing) to examine what is essential and where change might begin. For the programs that are working hard to improve the structures and systems that make it difficult for individual students to break the traditional mold, it can be helpful to learn about similar efforts, both to bolster the foundation for supporting such changes and to learn in advance from challenges that other programs have encountered. This cross-pollination is especially important given that the question of career diversity and professionalization can be most effectively addressed when considered alongside other pressing issues in graduate education. One program's focus on developing systematic professional development and individual support for graduate students can be strengthened and amplified by supporting like-minded programs that advocate for fair labor practices for contingent faculty members; by lobbying against the trend toward labor casualization and just-in-time hiring; or by working toward robust pedagogical support for both graduate students and faculty. All these efforts are necessary to building scholarly structures that support the best research and teaching while also strengthening individual outcomes.

Full support for doctoral students' career pathways entails not only offering opportunities for skill development but also encouraging a broader definition of what constitutes postgraduate success. While a number of initiatives, such as the Woodrow Wilson Foundation's Responsive PhD project (2000–2005),[8] have worked to shift university paradigms and encourage better career preparation for graduate students, their resulting methods and recommendations have still not been widely adopted. More recently, the report of the Modern Language Association's Task Force on Doctoral Education offered a suite of strong recommendations on reforming the humanities PhD,[9] and funding agencies including the National Endowment for the Humanities and the Mellon Foundation have stepped in to support such efforts. The MLA's report is still too recent to assess uptake and outcomes, but it signals the importance of doctoral education reform to the discipline as a whole, and provides a useful starting point for discussions that can lead to real action.

Why Pursue a PhD?

Before digging too deeply into how to prepare successfully for and transition into a meaningful career, it's worth stepping back to take a look at the purpose of rigorous academic study. Why do universities offer humanities PhDs in the first place? And why do people pursue them?

The pursuit of knowledge, the desire to better understand the world, the hope to contribute to learning and to create new meaning—all of these can be profound reasons that people pursue advanced studies in the humanities. In humanities disciplines, the doctoral degree is an opportunity for deep specialization as well as expansive thinking in the various forms of cultural expression and human experience that bring meaning to our lives. At its best, the standard structure of coursework, exams, and dissertation provides students with a model of decreasing structure that enables them to move progressively from a learner to an expert—and not only an expert, but one who can compellingly share that expertise with others. Comprehensive exams are the moment when doctoral students prove that they have a firm grasp on the thinkers who came before, while the long, unstructured deep dive of the dissertation gives them a chance to show that they can effectively craft, complete, and defend new interventions in their areas of study. This ongoing project of learning, inquiry, and articulation pushes the boundaries of long-established fields. Humanities fields need top-notch research by new experts in order to question the inclusion or exclusion of certain writers or artists from a broadly accepted canon; to consider marginalized perspectives and develop a more complex understanding of histories; to create compelling visions for where we, as humans, have been and where we are going.

An unstated purpose of graduate students' rigorous and creative work is to feed the knowledge they create back into the academy through both teaching and research.[10] But why should scholarship be confined to such a narrow space? Humanities study taps into some of the deepest motivations and fears of individuals and societies—how we understand identity and belonging; what we consider to be beautiful; how dynamics of power, authority, and rebellion change over time. These questions resonate with people far beyond the confines of the classroom, and rely on knowledge and cultural artifacts created both within and outside of the artificial constructs of disciplines or periodization. Without changing the rigor of study in the slightest, it is easy to imagine a very different breadth and depth of engagement with communities of practice and with various publics, both in the way students learn and in how and where they apply their expertise.

Pursuing a graduate degree in the humanities means undertaking a life of research that involves deep inquiry into areas of uncertainty—except, often, where professional outcomes are concerned. Whereas a student's research may take her through time, space, and varied paradigms, the end product almost invariably takes the form of an article or monograph, and the expectation for advancement is the steady progression from apprentice, to junior faculty member, to tenure. But why should the structures meant to train emerging scholars and foster academic freedom and inquiry limit the reach of brilliant people and their ideas in this way? While it is crucial that some scholars go on to continue their research and teaching in this traditional manner, expanding the range of scholarly products and career paths would mean huge gains for society, bringing new ideas to the public through a wide range of institutions. With deeper and more sustained public connection, the relevance of higher education would be more immediately apparent, prompting greater public support. Ideally, that support could then translate into stronger city and state investments, slowing the defunding process that is dismantling public higher education. Further, recognizing a broader range of what scholarly work can look like makes it possible for scholars with varied backgrounds and skill sets to break new ground. It opens up new avenues so that institutions aren't gatekeeping in the same ways, letting the same people advance all the time.

What Kinds of Careers?

The reasons that a graduate student or PhD holder might consider a career beyond the classroom vary widely. In many cases, the most significant step involves a shift in thinking about career opportunities as either "faculty" or "not-faculty" to instead seeing a faculty career as one option among many. Seen that way, it is far easier to assess the advantages and drawbacks of a faculty career in a neutral way, rather than through the lens of a deficit model that considers anything outside a narrowly defined norm to be less valuable.

Despite the wide range of career pathways graduates pursue, including those where they continue to teach and conduct research, professional development is not a routine component of many graduate programs. To the extent that career preparation is discussed, it is often with the expectation that successful completion of graduate work will automatically put one on a path toward a particular kind of success. Higher education continues to be one of the most promising indicators of future earnings, so it is with good reason that many expect graduate study to lead to stable, fulfilling careers. While a faculty position involving some combination of teaching and research remains the most common path for people with doctoral degrees in humanities fields,[11] it is far from the only possibility.

Moving outward from an academic department, career possibilities might include staff or hybrid work in universities—careers in administration, libraries, humanities centers, or student services, for instance. But the higher education universe doesn't end at the boundaries of the university's campus. Many other institutions also support the structure of higher education and can be excellent places of employment. These include scholarly societies, professional associations, publishers, state and federal governmental agencies, and policy organizations. Radiating further from the university are institutions that promote public learning and knowledge sharing: museums, archives, public libraries, cultural heritage organizations, the media, performing arts, cultural and educational nonprofits, and many more. And for companies directly related to education or cultural heritage—anything from educational technology companies to tourism-related industries—humanities expertise is incredibly valuable. Even companies without a clear connection to the humanities in their mission can have engaging and relevant opportunities in areas like research and development; tech companies, for instance, face a multitude of ethical and intercultural questions and have increasingly turned to humanities scholars to help them think differently about how their products will function in the world. Independent consulting and freelancing is an attractive option for some, and others apply the skills gained in graduate school to careers far afield from the subject matter of their discipline. Not all of these jobs *require* PhDs, of course, and there is some concern about encouraging people with doctorates into careers that have typically been pathways for people with master's degrees. While this kind of "credential creep" is a valid concern, for the most part the benefits of encouraging highly trained humanities practitioners to pursue broader career goals far outweigh the potential drawbacks. For the purposes of this book, I focus specifically on doctoral programs and people with PhDs, since a discussion of similar topics for master's programs would merit another book's worth of analysis.

The Current Landscape: Career Expectations

When I conducted the "Humanities Unbound" study, a few clear patterns stood out.[12] First, there was very little diversity of career goals at the outset of graduate work. Respondents reported that when they began their studies, they did so with the overwhelming goal of eventually becoming faculty members. Most felt highly confident about this future pathway.[13] These numbers are particularly striking because the survey targeted people with careers outside the professoriate.[14] Instead of working as faculty members as they had anticipated doing, these survey participants were employed at a number of different types of workplaces, with a large majority working within universities, libraries, and other cultural heritage organizations. The data shows that, historically, many graduate students have begun their studies without a clear understanding of their future employment prospects. While the degree of transparency about the likelihood of obtaining a tenure-track position may have improved in recent years, overall the responses signal that we are failing to bring informed students into the graduate education system.

Deepening the problem, students reported receiving little or no preparation for careers outside the professoriate during the course of their studies, even though the need for information about a variety of careers is acute. Only 18 percent reported feeling satisfied or very satisfied with the preparation they received for careers outside the classroom. The responses were rooted in perception, so there may have been resources available that students were not taking advantage of—but whatever the reason, they did not feel that they were being adequately prepared. That perception reveals significant room for improvement throughout the higher education system. Further, if programs devote time and funding to resources for career preparation, it is essential to offer and promote them from the very beginning of graduate students' careers. Failing to do so may limit the effectiveness of such interventions, since it reinstates the sense that a career beyond the classroom is a "plan B" that is less prestigious than a faculty position would be. Students are very good at sensing implicit signals from their peers and advisors, which is one reason that it is crucial to embed the discussions in the earliest stages of graduate school as students are getting their footing in a program.

People reported pursuing nonfaculty jobs for reasons ranging from the practical and immediate—salary, benefits, family considerations—to more future- and goal-oriented reasons, such as the desire to gain new skills, contribute to society, and advance in one's career. While there are a great many reasons for pursuing one career or another, one of the key factors in opting for something other than a faculty career is the desire for geographic flexibility and control. Faculty careers often require a regional or national search and one or more relocations before settling into a long-term position, and sometimes the towns and cities where universities are located offer few opportunities for partners who may also be seeking work. Moreover, some college locations—for instance, small towns whose populations are overwhelmingly white, or states with transphobic laws in place—may not be safe or hospitable environments for all jobseekers. Broadening the career search to other types of positions makes it far easier for a person to control where they live. Another major reason is flexibility and career advancement. Even though academic freedom is one of the strongest draws of a faculty position, for some people a faculty career feels limiting. Pursuing other options allows an individual to develop new skills, seek out unexpected opportunities, and push themselves in ways they may not have done. The desire for greater freedom, or simply a different environment than a university department, appealed to many. One respondent cited the prospect of "an interesting job in a field where wide-ranging intellectual curiosity is an asset" to be a very important reason for pursuing their chosen career. Another mentioned the "tremendous autonomy" their chosen position offered. Much more simply, though, a large number of respondents cited the need to find a stable job as their primary motivation. Some respondents considered themselves "overwhelmed," "burned out," or "frustrated."[15] A note of urgency and, sometimes, desperation came through in a number of these responses.

What all of this information underscores is that a critical consideration of the ways we talk about work—whether as a faculty member or in any number of careers beyond the classroom—is an important step for graduate students to gain more realistic expectations and clearer understandings of their own strengths, needs, and desires. Until we talk about faculty work in the language of labor and employment, it will remain shrouded in mystique that makes it difficult for graduate students to consider it as one option among many.

Many positions that involve translating humanities study into a broader public good are a part of the growing discourse of "alt-academic" careers, a category that is both hard to define and nearly impossible to measure accurately. The changing nature of career paths for humanities scholars is an issue of particular concern to digital humanities practitioners, who have long been working in hybrid roles that combine elements of traditional scholarship, like research and teaching, with other elements, such as software development, librarianship, high-level administrative responsibilities, and more. These roles are not new, but the term reflected an effort on the part of the scholarly community to find a unified and elegant way to refer to such careers. Many of the skills implicit in digital humanities scholarship and work products—including collaboration, project management, and technological fluency—are becoming increasingly important in new models of graduate training, even among programs not specifically allied with the digital humanities. The spheres of alt-academic careers and the digital humanities can be best understood as a Venn diagram, with significant areas of overlap as well as distinctive qualities. Many fruitful conversations and initiatives related to broadening career paths have emerged from the digital humanities community, and there are important reasons why this is the case. At the same time, the two areas are not identical; many digital humanists work as tenured and tenure-track professors, while many who identify as working in alternative academic roles do not engage in the kinds of scholarship or practice associated with the digital humanities.

While the scope of the alt-academic umbrella is a topic of a great deal of conversation and some contention, it is also possible—and perhaps more productive—to take a broad view that is defined not so much by the specific job or career, but rather by a type of approach or lens. The most compelling common denominator among people who have adopted the "alt-academic" moniker is that they tend to see their work through the lens of academic training, and incorporate scholarly methods into the way that work is done. They engage in work with the same intellectual curiosity that fueled the desire to go to graduate school in the first place, and apply the same kinds of skills—such as close reading, historical inquiry, or written argumentation—to the tasks at hand. This kind of fluid definition encourages us to seek out the unexpected places where people are finding their intellectual curiosity piqued and their research skills tested and sharpened.

This kind of engagement occurs in the classroom, but also in a wide range of other work environments. One commonality across many career paths is that in addition to the intellectual challenges, there are also many other challenges that draw on different kinds of skills. Some jobs require excellent management skills; others require marketing or sales skills; still others require technical skills. These are not often gained as part of the core curriculum in graduate school—but then, neither are the skills required to be an excellent teacher, administrator, grant writer, and faculty colleague. The intellectual and interpretive skills acquired in graduate programs span many careers. The other essential skills vary, and are often learned on the job—and people may find some appealing while disliking others. It is often these ancillary skills that make someone seem "suited" for one particular career or another. A good guiding question for someone wondering what this looks like in practicality is, what are the kinds of problems you like to solve? The challenges of teaching—the constraints of the physical classroom, the institutional structures that govern a course's size and meeting time, the performative nature of some modes of teaching—may not be the kinds of challenges that a scholar likes to undertake. Instead, someone may feel stimulated by the problem-solving involved in other types of work, such as working to change institutional structures, making connections and partnerships, pitching ideas, writing to different audiences, building a client base, and more. The key is rethinking the way we understand intellectual labor and how we see it embedded in many kinds of work. The rhythms and routines of faculty careers are well worn. It is time to think more creatively about where and how scholarly expertise can be applied.

Career Diversity Is Good for the Academy, Too

It is time to go beyond an oppositional model that defines careers by what they are not. Even though the notion of an "alt-academy" was intended as a reimagining of what is traditionally accepted as scholarly work, in just a few short years it has become reinscribed in the binary of faculty and nonfaculty labor. The same is true of other formulations: postacademic, nonacademic, and so on. With powerful norms governing expectations, it is difficult to break out of this tendency to define against the default. How can we, instead, think both within and beyond the existing structures and work to redefine them in a way that makes the default far more expansive? I will undertake this challenge in the chapters that follow by addressing not only preparation for careers beyond the classroom but also labor issues and questions of preparation and training for faculty careers. By first understanding the ways in which graduate programs do not always do well what they are expected to do—that is, prepare emerging scholars to become the next generation of faculty members—the opportunities for improvement along multiple axes will become more apparent. Better career preparation isn't something that is needed on the margins of doctoral education; it is needed at the core. The current norms of graduate training often appear to be a failed apprenticeship model—preparing students for just one career path, but not preparing them particularly well, and without acknowledging the long odds of gaining a foothold in the field.

A key factor that is often overlooked in discussions about professionalization is this: all of the elements that make stronger employees are also greatly beneficial for those grads that do go on to become professors. In other words, preparing well for careers beyond the classroom is an excellent way of sharpening your teaching, research, and writing skills as well. Research, teaching, collaboration, project management, problem solving: each of these skills is something that is as valuable in the classroom as it is in a nonprofit, cultural heritage organization, or company. In an analysis of job ads published in the Modern Language Association's Jobs Information List, Beth Seltzer, Roopika Risam, and Matt Applegate found that many faculty job listings expressed the desirability of skills that might be more commonly thought of as belonging to the worlds of administration or management.[16] For example, project management skills can help students to complete their dissertations and conduct research in a more effective and timely manner, and are also a crucial component of developing and teaching a course.

The notion that preparing students for varied careers somehow detracts from their core formation as scholars is simply false. Rather, the kinds of interventions that equip students to succeed in a wide range of job settings can also help them to be effective in their teaching and research if they do become faculty members. Understanding how graduate work can be applicable to different careers helps lay the foundations for students to translate their studies into different contexts, rather than suggesting that what they are learning is only valuable within the university itself. The result may be more meaningful research that can effectively reach a wide range of audiences, and a nuanced approach to understanding the world that can be applied in any professional context.

Overview of the Book

The complex backdrop that underpins graduate study is too often invisible to students as they begin their doctoral work. In *Putting the Humanities PhD to Work*, I aim to demystify this institutional context while also teasing out connections among seemingly distinct elements. I will begin with a broad view of the higher education landscape and the stakes of the career diversity movement, with special focus on why this can be understood as a social justice project. Then, I will build on that foundation to offer concrete suggestions for advisors and students—advice that is grounded in the idea that a broader understanding of scholarly success is structurally as well as individually valuable.

Chapter 1 offers background and context and lays a foundation for the book's argument that a broader understanding of postgraduate success is good for individuals, the academy, and society. In "The Academic Workforce: Expectations and Realities," I examine academic labor structures, including both tenure-track faculty careers and adjunct positions. I also consider the ways that the apprenticeship model of graduate study creates strong incentives and cultural expectations that students will become professors. The chapter addresses what is perhaps the single most damaging practice facing higher education today: the increasing reliance on underpaid, overworked adjunct faculty members with limited rights and resources. I begin here because it is essential to understand the current system in all its limitations before exploring new opportunities and different mind-sets. After examining the current landscape, including the systemic and institutional reasons that tenure-track job opportunities have become so difficult to obtain despite the high demand for the humanities at the undergraduate level, I discuss the expectations that many graduate students have when they enter their programs (spoiler alert: a faculty career), and why the current state of faculty labor should prompt us to look beyond the classroom.

Chapters 2 and 3 focus on the ways that developing a broader definition of scholarly success is an essential social justice issue, and an important step toward rebuilding trust and investment in higher education as a public good. Chapter 2, "Inclusive Systems, Vibrant Scholarship," examines the ways that current university practices, including the implicit signals and markers of prestige that are commonplace in graduate programs, perpetuate systems of inequality that result in the continued underrepresentation of women of all races and ethnicities and minorities of all genders in the academy. As an example, I examine institutional diversity efforts that push to increase the numbers of people from underrepresented groups yet fail because they do not address broader issues of departmental climate or bias. After a consideration of the academy's conservative nature—which rewards those whose achievements map onto a narrow definition of success—I argue that a broader understanding of scholarly success that includes innovative and applied research may support both broader career pathways and a more truly inclusive university environment.

In chapter 3, "Expanding Definitions of Scholarly Success," I look specifically at innovative scholarly work and the potential it creates for deeper connections with various communities within and beyond the university. As scholars and technologists create new platforms and structures for sharing research, there are increased opportunities for that work to have a meaningful impact that goes far beyond the reach of a traditional peer-reviewed journal article. However, if scholars are to devote their time and resources to sharing their work through innovative or experimental channels, there must be professional recognition for doing so. From digital dissertations to network building and from policy-relevant research to activist community engagement, greater flexibility in what is understood by the academy to constitute valuable research would help cultivate stronger public understanding of, and support for, systems of higher education.

The ideas and arguments of the first three chapters form a solid foundation on which I build a proposed action plan: concrete strategies that all readers can implement in order to work toward a more inclusive and public-oriented model of graduate education that embraces career diversity. The fourth chapter, "What Faculty and Advisors Can Do," provides practical, action-oriented suggestions for faculty members and program directors. The ideas in this chapter are intended to help individual advisors as well as humanities departments improve the ways they implicitly and explicitly support their students and alumni. These elements include advising, curricular reform, professional development opportunities, messages about what is valued, and more. The chapter offers suggestions for individual mentorship as well as possibilities for broader programmatic change, with both immediate and long-term opportunities for reform. But the chapter is not only for faculty members or senior administrators; students will find the advice in this chapter grounds them in their own approach while providing a valuable starting point for discussion with their own advisors and peers.

Finally, chapter 5, "Students: How to Put Your PhD to Work," continues this action plan with a focus on what students need, offering theoretical analyses, case studies, and suggestions on how to move from experimentation to implementation. Faculty members will want to take special note of this chapter as well, since it may influence their own approaches not only to mentorship and advising but also to teaching, program structure, and more. The chapter offers practical research-based suggestions and examples of individual and institutional success stories designed to help readers strategize their own futures in a realistic and meaningful way. For individuals, this requires grasping the realities that exist, thinking through the options that are possible given those opportunities and constraints, formulating a flexible but concrete plan, and, at the same time, working toward broader institutional change. Few students have comprehensive guidance on all of those fronts at once; this book can help to fill in the gaps in a way that keeps students' complex lives—their commitments, goals, desires, fears, lived realities, and concrete needs—in mind. As a final take-away, the book concludes with ten concrete ways to get started.

Throughout the book I explore how rhetoric and practices related to career preparation are evolving, and how those changes intersect with admissions practices, scholarly reward structures, and academic labor practices. Consideration of the stakes of such discussions—including the effects of increasing reliance on adjunct and contingent faculty labor, the size of graduate programs and the support they provide to their students, and the relationship between career expectations and systemic issues of diversity in higher education—are a constant undercurrent. The challenges are real, and complex; everything from small individual steps to major reform efforts are essential. Whether you are a student shaping your own pathway, a faculty member guiding students, or an administrator building or refining a program, there are things you can do today to support career diversity, increase the impact of humanities research, and bolster public investment in higher education. As University of Michigan professor and past president of the Modern Language Association Sidonie Smith writes in her *Manifesto for the Humanities: Transforming Doctoral Education in Good Enough Times*, "'the times are good enough' to transform doctoral education in the humanities."[17] This framing presents optimism and solace, but also a call to urgency: the time to act is not some hypothetical future day, but now, with the resources and challenges we have today. In short, this is a noncynical approach to the realities of the humanities PhD that offers practical career advice, opportunities for reform, and an affirmation of humanities education as a public good.

The Academic Workforce: Expectations and Realities

"Are you sure you want to finish?" The words hung in the air as I slowly digested the question my academic program coordinator, Patricia Paige, was asking. Of *course* I wanted to finish. It hadn't even occurred to me to stop short of my goal of a doctoral degree. It was 2007, and we were speaking by phone; I was in France, spending the year teaching English to middle schoolers while preparing for my comprehensive exams. By all measures, I was doing very well in my program. But teaching—especially teaching eleven- to fourteen-year-olds, as I was doing that year—drained me, and left me feeling lonely and isolated. This was before the 2008 financial crash hit and added even more pressure to university budgets, but even then, I didn't really want to pursue a faculty career. Why keep pushing through the work of a PhD if I didn't see myself on that path? Paige's question was one that I had not asked myself once I was embedded in my doctoral program.

The conversation was clarifying. More than anything, it reminded me that I did indeed have a choice in determining what was best for me, and that what that looked like might change over time. That finishing a doctoral degree was not a necessary thing, and that I had already learned an enormous amount. That while I had funding, it wasn't much; I could earn more, build up experience, and start figuring out my future pathway more readily if I transitioned into full-time employment. And yet, even though I already suspected that a faculty career was not for me, I also sensed that seeing my goal through to completion would be valuable in ways I might not anticipate. When I decided that, yes, I would proceed to take my comps and write my dissertation, I felt empowered knowing that doing so was my decision. And yet I had no idea what the future would hold.

Even though I was fortunate to have a supportive dissertation advisor, the career guidance I received from faculty in my program—and even from my institution's career center—was extremely limited, which left me feeling like I was making decisions in the dark. This is not an uncommon story. Although there are numerous graduate career centers and other career-oriented initiatives in doctoral programs today, too many students continue to feel the same ambivalence and uncertainty that I felt: not necessarily wanting a faculty job (or wanting one but not confident that it will come to fruition), yet deeply committed to their doctoral work, and unsure of how to proceed. For countless others, a faculty career is what they have long imagined and prepared for, and yet the chances of landing a tenure-track position feel slim at best.

Understanding the current landscape of the modern gig economy—and especially the ways it manifests in the academic workforce—is a critical backdrop for the discussion about career preparation for doctoral students. This is not a cheerful way to begin the book; workforce casualization is a hallmark of the gig economy that characterizes labor structures across every sector, from retail and food service to education and medicine. Adjunct labor is a huge and complex problem in universities today, and one that affects students and faculty alike. But cheerful or not, a clear-sighted look at the current reality is a necessary starting point to reform. Only by knowing the current state of affairs is it possible to understand how various structural elements affect one another, and what the implications are for graduates' career prospects. Before I turn to broader professional opportunities and ideas for reform in later chapters, I'll focus here on the current status of teaching careers, including the tendency at many institutions to overemphasize the importance of research—which often correlates with a devaluation of teaching. I will argue that this value system is one factor in the rapid increase in adjunct teaching roles and in fostering the institutional structures that support a deeply unequal system, and that reform efforts must begin by reinvesting in the importance of teaching.

There are three key reasons why a discussion of the academic workforce matters in the context of this book:

→ First, it provides grounding for students to better understand the structures around them so that they can make informed decisions about their futures. Graduate students have a complex role within the university as learners, researchers, and often teachers. And yet that deep involvement coupled with many students' love of learning and of the classroom can make it difficult to conduct a clear-eyed career search, and leave students vulnerable to low wages and poor working conditions. Having more information makes it easier for students to advocate for themselves.

$\rightarrow$ Second, on an institutional level, I hope to convey that the solution to the labor crisis is not simply a matter of arithmetic—that is, reducing the size of humanities doctoral programs so that there are fewer new PhDs seeking faculty positions. Instead, truly addressing the issue requires a radical reinvestment in both teaching and the broad importance of the humanities. In this way I hope to show that the project of career diversity cannot be considered in isolation, but rather is one component of a broader reform framework that aims to strengthen and support the vibrant work of doctoral education.

$\rightarrow$ Finally, I hope to show that reinvesting in the importance and value of teaching is in no way at odds with the goal of opening up new career pathways for students. My approach to doctoral education reform comes from a deep respect for institutions of higher education, and from a desire to see those institutions become the best possible versions of themselves. To convince students—and the public—of the importance of education, colleges and universities must demonstrate respect for the profession of teaching through material support. This begins with labor practices.

Expectations: The Problem of Love

One precondition to the current academic labor structure has to do with the deeply held career expectations that many students have (or are subtly encouraged to adopt) when they begin their doctoral work. The deep commitment that people may have to their research area, to education in general, and to the idea of teaching the next generation of students can create a blind spot where labor conditions are concerned. A rhetoric of vocation and even love often suffuses the conversation about teaching and scholarly work more broadly—people feel a sense of calling to do this kind of work. Many faculty members love what they do, and will say so openly. And yet, as numerous scholars including Fred Moten, Stefano Harney, Michael Bérubé, and Kathi Inman Berens have all described, the notion that one works "for love" reflects a position of privilege that minimizes the struggle many academics face to support themselves, and renders invisible the barriers that exacerbate the challenges for women, people of color, people with disabilities, and others who are not well supported by the structures of academe.[1] Berens's reflection on the topic at the 2013 Digital Humanities conference was partly in reaction to earlier remarks by the keynote speaker at the same conference, Willard McCarty, who had confessed to doing his work purely out of love.[2] What a wonderful thing, to work purely for love! And yet it requires a high degree of both luck and privilege to both work for love and earn a living (or to have no need to earn a living). Such a happenstance approach is all but impossible for those who are less likely to be recognized and validated by the mechanisms of the academy.

Emphasizing love in a context of labor is a tidy way of de-emphasizing things like wages, benefits, and working conditions—the material realities that, because they relate to bodies, seem somehow beneath the so-called life of the mind. Moten and Harney describe the way those who "teach for food" serve as the university's undercommons, necessary but despised. Working in this manner differs from the challenging rites of passage of doctoral study itself, in that it is not something that is simply passed through on the way to something better: "The moment of teaching for food is therefore often mistakenly taken to be a stage, as if eventually, one should not teach for food."[3] In some cases, the mentality of working for love rather than for sustenance renders crass any discussion about postgraduate employment, as though those who pursue knowledge for its own sake need not worry about financial stability, access to health care, and retirement savings. But in an economic climate where unemployment is high across all sectors, the issue of future employment is not something that can be taken for granted.

This rhetoric of love is one of the mechanisms that can lead people to endure underemployment, insufficient wages, and poor working conditions. Many persist—understandably—in wanting to do what they love despite these drawbacks. Academia has socialized scholars to think that any focus on a salary, benefits, even the location where one lives, is crass—even though all of these material realities have a major impact on health and well-being, and would be central to job considerations in almost any other field. The effect of this mind-set is an undervaluation of the actual labor of teaching and research, which is not only detrimental to individuals but also diminishes the public's perception of the profession. This combination—the emphasis on love and the lack of acknowledgment of the embodied realities of work—has been deeply damaging to the institution of higher education. By casting teaching and research not as work—

part of a capitalist labor economy—but rather as a noble calling, the possibility of exploitation is much increased. The risk of not having health insurance is significant for anyone, and can be particularly devastating to people with disabilities, other health considerations, caregiving responsibilities, or even the simple desire to start a family one day—and love has nothing to do with it.

Scholars who are women, people of color, people who identify as LGBTQ+, and members of other underrepresented groups are highly susceptible to this dangerous rhetorical move. For instance, scholars in minority categories often shoulder a heavier burden of service work—serving on diversity committees and providing mentorship and guidance as they work to bring the margins into the center—while also receiving fewer material and prestige-oriented benefits from their labor. In other words, the lack of a promotion or other clear and valued recognition may be justified by telling the scholar that they should be "doing it for love," placing the burden of repairing the discipline on them without rewarding them in the coin of the realm. This is one reason it is crucial to talk about ability, health, race, ethnicity, gender, and sexuality when talking about academic and scholarly labor. Rendering invisible factors that have deep and lasting effects on an individual's ability to thrive in the field victimizes vulnerable scholars a second time, by falsely claiming there are only individual rather than systemic elements at play.

Reality: Labor Conditions

The idea that the life of the mind is somehow separate and independent from physical well-being is most often rooted in the privilege of material security. To be sure, the pleasure of pursuing knowledge is one of the deep satisfactions of advanced graduate study—but scholars still have to make rent. Discussions about careers and career preparation can sometimes be derailed by the idea that graduate education would be somehow diluted by thinking about such preparation, but PhD programs that gloss over the realities of postgraduate employment do their students a disservice. Part of the worry seems to be that doctoral study will become overly vocational in its approach; and yet such a position misses the current reality that graduate school is *already* a vocational model—but for a single, narrow profession into which not all graduates will go. Doctoral education in its current state could be described as reproductive: faculty members train students to do the specific thing that they are doing, and once today's grad students become tomorrow's professors, the cycle repeats.[4] However, even in this narrow set of goals it cannot be said that most institutions are particularly successful, given that the professional development that students receive is often mediocre at best. With minimal preparation and a limited view of the systems and structures that affect academic employment, more and more PhDs are finding that when they try to take the next steps within that professional cycle, they are instead getting stuck cobbling together courses to teach on short-term contracts with no benefits.

The Current Landscape

The fact that the story of getting stuck on the adjunct track is so common is a sign that it is rooted in structural failings rather than individual factors. And, in fact, perhaps the single greatest threat to the integrity and health of higher education is the increasing reliance on short-term adjunct instructors. According to the American Association of University Professors (AAUP), non-tenure-track appointments now constitute 70 percent of the instructional workforce.[5] This is a bit of a slippery figure; the ways that adjunct positions are counted varies by institution, making it difficult to compare over time or across location. For instance, the AAUP's figure includes graduate assistants, who comprise 13 percent of the instructional workforce. Whether graduate student labor should be counted in the same way as adjunct faculty labor is a point of contention, given that graduate students are simultaneously learners and workers. The National Labor Relations Board's 2016 ruling that graduate students are indeed employees suggests that including them in the tally is justifiable.[6] At the same time, because graduate assistantships are structured and compensated so differently across institutions, it is difficult to determine the degree to which the assistantship serves primarily as part of the student's own formative training versus as an institutional stop-gap measure to meet labor needs. Moreover, the AAUP's number includes both part-time and full-time instructors, and does not differentiate by credential, which is an issue since not all adjunct instructors hold PhDs. Motivation is also impossible to see in this figure; one study showed that about a quarter of adjuncts would not seek a full-time tenure-track job even if one was available.[7]

Even with these caveats, 70 percent is an incredibly high number. And regardless of how the counting is done, the structure of contingent positions creates clear issues for nearly all adjuncts: low wages, instability, and a lack of supportive structures. This is not only the case in colleges and universities; across many industries, from journalism to retail to the service industry, today's workforce is subject to the whims of the gig economy, with workers in both high- and low-skilled fields cobbling together jobs and wages to make ends meet when stable and consistent employment proves elusive. Thanks to the work of Joshua Boldt, who started the Adjunct Project to document the compensation of adjunct faculty members, we now know that most of these instructors receive less than $3,000 per course.[8] As a point of reference, the Modern Language Association has recommended that colleges pay adjuncts no less than $10,900 per three-credit course.[9] Tell this to an adjunct, and they will laugh (and cry)—that number seems like pure fiction for most. Consequently, many adjuncts teach heavy loads just to make ends meet, often five or more courses per semester, sometimes at multiple institutions, stretching them thin and leaving little time for preparation, assessment, and advising.

How much is lost when brilliant students and lecturers are unsupported by the system? Shannon Reed took a comedic approach in her satirical piece in *McSweeney's*, "Classic College Movies Updated for the Adjunct Era." Satirizing a number of films set in and around colleges and universities, the piece recasts brilliant characters as adjuncts whose potential is utterly undermined by the impossibility of securing a stable foundation for their work (that is, a tenure-track faculty position). The synopsis for a reimagined *Good Will Hunting*, for instance, ends unhappily for all:

> MIT Professor Gerald Lambeau is impressed by the intellect of Will Hunting, a janitor who solved an extremely difficult math problem, but Will needs help processing his complex emotions and anger. Lambeau turns to his estranged former college roommate, Dr. Sean Maguire, for help. Sadly, Maguire, an adjunct professor who must shuttle between three campuses in two states and teach 7 classes a semester to stay off the dole, can't find a minute to call Lambeau back. Will ends up in jail by the age of 23, Lambeau never goes out on a limb for another student, and Maguire is fired for being late to class because of a car pile-up on I-90.[10]

The negative personal outcomes in this satirical scenario are obvious (risk aversion, joblessness, even incarceration). Less visible is the impact on scholarship and society, but that follows close behind: when people with tremendous potential are unable to find their footing, that potential never comes to fruition. As the number of success stories diminishes (within a certain definition of success), it becomes less and less likely that programs will take risks, either on people who may not have a clear academic pedigree or on truly innovative research. Universities become places where only the most conventional cases lead to success, and where research progresses slowly not because of great care, but because the risk-to-reward ratio has become too steep.

The increasingly tough odds of the academic job market are not due to decreased interest in the humanities. On the contrary, undergraduate humanities course enrollments remain high (despite a recent decline in the number of humanities majors). In fact, the need for humanities instructors has continued to grow in recent years. However, the number of new tenure-track positions in the humanities has remained relatively flat.[11] To meet the demand for course instruction, the overall number of people teaching college-level humanities courses is increasing significantly—but, more and more, the increasing numbers are made up of adjuncts, not full-time hires, which drives the changing proportion of part-time faculty. Rapid growth in student enrollment alongside uncertainty about the number of majors may in fact be one reason for adding adjuncts to a teaching roster, since they can be engaged without a lengthy search process or complicated human resources protocols. But they're not being hired only in a pinch; instead, adjuncts have become a fixture of higher education. Students may not understand the difference in the employment circumstances of their professors—I certainly didn't—and, yet, those circumstances have a powerful effect on student learning conditions.

For instance, adjuncts often teach introductory courses, when students are new and vulnerable. These introductory courses are among the most challenging to teach from a pedagogical perspective, as they require deft translation of complex methods and content into language and concepts effective for teaching students encountering the subject for the first time. Moreover, many of these students are also encountering college for the first time, and they are learning not only subject matter but also college readiness. All of this requires more intensive time and attention from faculty members. To maximize student retention and success, universities should be offering significant support to faculty members assigned to teach introductory courses. And yet universities tend to go in the opposite direction, with contract employees assigned to teach introductory courses and tenured faculty teaching upper-division or graduate-level courses. Many of these adjunct faculty members have abundant experience and bring exceptional teaching skills to the classroom; however, their positions typically offer the bare minimum of institutional support, which does a disservice to both the faculty members and the students. Such support could take different forms; a start would be reasonable teaching schedules, higher compensation, multiyear contracts, opportunities for professional development (such as support for conference and research travel)—and, at a bare minimum, consistent access to office space and basic equipment.[12]

These material realities affect the ways that adjuncts can do their jobs, and they risk negatively affecting student learning outcomes because adjuncts often have minimal time or space for mentoring, advising, and providing the guidance that can help students to excel. Even planning lessons and evaluating student work are challenging when compensation is so low. Non-tenure-track faculty are often paid so little that it is difficult for them to continue to advance professionally through research, conferences, and so on, which creates a cycle that is incredibly difficult to break. The most important refrain of the adjunct activism movement, and the one that is most likely to lead to change, is that faculty working conditions are student learning conditions. Despite abundant training and often exceptional teaching skills, the lack of institutional support, reasonable salaries, and benefits can curtail adjunct faculty's effectiveness and undermine their expertise. Indeed, in the (all too rare) cases where this support is present, adjuncts are found to be highly effective and devoted teachers.

For instance, a study by David N. Figlio, Morton O. Schapiro, and Kevin B. Soter showed that non-tenure-track faculty members at Northwestern University actually achieved better student learning outcomes in first-year courses than their tenure-track colleagues.[13] The study was met with surprise and some skepticism, but given the way that Northwestern structures these instructional positions, the results make quite a bit of sense. Adjuncts at Northwestern earn unusually high wages relative to peer institutions, and also benefit from strong professional support.[14] The study thus implicitly showed that material working conditions affect student outcomes, and that bolstering support for adjuncts can improve student learning conditions. However, the unusually high level of support for adjuncts at Northwestern relative to other institutions also means that the results are anomalous and cannot be broadly applied without controlling for the wage differential encountered at most other colleges and universities. Even so, the study affirms what so many know to be true—that adjunct faculty members are very well equipped to teach in terms of their education and training. I would argue that the study also showed something that it did not intend to reveal: that valuing adjunct labor produces strong student results. If a key goal of colleges and universities is to educate students, then the ways that labor conditions affect student outcomes should be of central importance.

In addition to its effects on student learning conditions, the increasing use of adjuncts also negatively affects shared governance—an essential tenet of the tenure system and academic freedom—and the workloads of tenure-line faculty members. As Michael Bérubé and Jennifer Ruth explore in depth in *The Humanities, Higher Education, and Academic Freedom: Three Necessary Arguments* (2015), the swelling ranks of adjuncts affects overall shared governance in at least two ways. First, the casual hiring process of adjuncts—often done at the last minute and with minimal oversight—undermines the careful hiring process driven by peer evaluation that tenure-line faculty members undergo. The makeup of the community therefore changes in a way that the community itself has not necessarily authorized. Moreover, because adjuncts are subject to hiring and firing with little notice, they are not in a position to weigh in candidly on matters affecting the department—especially on matters like course enrollments and curricular changes that may affect the likelihood that their employment will continue.

Research is also profoundly affected by the increasing reliance on contingent labor, though this effect is perhaps less visible than that on teaching or governance. In the humanities, the impact of precarious employment on research hinges mainly on the absence of time and support for research and writing, but in the sciences the impact on research is more direct. While most contingent positions in the humanities are teaching-focused, postdocs in the sciences are generally research-driven. Much like adjunct lecturer appointments in the humanities, short-term postdoctoral positions are on the rise in the sciences,[15] and the effects on research output are becoming more and more visible.

The lack of support means fewer people must do more with less, which also leads to increased pressure, burnout, and errors. This is true not only in the humanities, but across all disciplines, including the bench sciences. As Brenda Iasevoli reports in *NPREd*, the increasing reliance on postdocs for lab research—and the decreasing support that those postdocs receive—is directly affecting the quality of research.[16] In the article, biology PhD Gary McDowell notes that there are a rising number of article retractions, a shift he attributes to researchers altering data in the face of the increasing pressure of the academic job market. The United Kingdom bioethics report he uses to support his claim also suggests that senior scientists may not have enough time to devote to training junior researchers in best practices.[17] Echoing this claim, a recent joint report from the National Academy of Sciences, National Academy of Engineering, and Institute of Medicine argues both for better pay and stronger mentorship of postdocs in order to improve the quality of training that they receive as they enter the medical profession.[18] Without supportive structures and opportunities for systematic professional development, recent PhDs are left to sink or swim both in the classroom and in the lab.

New Faculty Majority, New Student Majority

Adjuncts have become the "New Faculty Majority," with around three-quarters of instructors working outside of tenure-line positions.[19] This shift is taking place at precisely the same time that colleges are experiencing a demographic shift resulting in a "new majority" of college students: while mainstream media often depicts college students as eighteen- to twenty-two-year-olds attending residential colleges far from home, in fact more than half of students enrolled in undergraduate programs in the United States are enrolled in community colleges, and many are older, having returned after years working or raising kids. Many attend part-time and balance obligations including work and family responsibilities. They are often the first in their families to attend college, and many identify with historically underrepresented groups. These major changes in the composition of the student body as well as the faculty mean that there are, in fact, a wealth of opportunities in higher education that are often over-looked, especially in community colleges. For students who feel called to teach and who long to make a difference, community college teaching is a powerful way to channel expertise into a meaningful career at an institution that values access and success for all students, not selectivity and elitism for only a few. Advisors may not encourage their students to pursue community college posi-tions because of the perceived lack of prestige of such positions. And, because many graduate programs do not adequately train their students to teach, com-munity colleges are often skeptical of recent grad students who, they fear, may bail on the position once the exigencies of the job become apparent. And those demands are real: as one example, until recently faculty at the CUNY commu-nity colleges taught nine courses annually, with many service expectations, so fitting in any research time was hard—even though research is required for tenure.[20] While there is no robust data showing average current teaching loads across the country, this schedule appears typical for community college faculty members nationwide.[21] But for those who love to teach and who want to teach where they can have the greatest impact, community colleges are an appealing opportunity.

And yet at both the community college and comprehensive or senior col-lege level, the shift from tenure-track to adjunct positions has eroded the most central structures and values of higher education, such as shared governance and academic freedom. This growing reliance on instructional staff that are engaged on a course-by-course or term-by-term basis has created the sharply unequal work structure that remains largely invisible to students. In the class-room, students see their instructor and regardless of this person's teaching style—whether engaged or disconnected, someone with high standards or an "easy A"—the baseline understanding is that it is someone with the training and expertise to give them authority in the classroom. But students may have little idea of what happens between classes. If their professor is tenured or on the tenure track, she may return to her office, where she will hold office hours, prepare for another class, work on a bit of writing, or gather her thoughts before a committee meeting. An adjunct instructor, on the other hand, may rush out of class to head straight into teaching another class, perhaps on a different campus. She may arrange to meet students at a nearby coffee shop, since she has no office space for a private meeting. She may run by the library to make photocopies, since she may not have access to a copier within her department. She carries everything in a heavy bag since she has no space to drop off materials for one class before heading into the next. She doesn't go to committee meetings (or she goes and sits in silence), because her voice is not part of the structure of shared governance that makes decisions for the department.

Students don't often see the different kinds of work and challenges that their professors face outside of the class they are taking. And when they seek recommendations or advisement, they may turn with equal eagerness toward their full-time professors as to their adjunct instructors without differentiation. And yet adjunct instructors are typically not compensated for advisement, probably cannot oversee a thesis project, and their voices carry less weight in letters of recommendation. Further, with no guaranteed contract, they may be a valued mentor one year and gone from the institution the next.

The description above focuses mostly on the relationship between faculty and undergraduate students. Graduate students occupy a liminal space within this two-tier system. If they are teaching, it is most likely as part of a funding package that also includes a tuition waiver and other benefits. They are professors-in-training, not yet initiated into the ranks of tenure-track faculty and so perhaps unaware of the service, advising, and other ancillary duties that go along with a faculty career. But even if they have no office space to call their own, they most likely have at least some material or in-kind support that adjuncts do not, if only because their departments have invested more resources in their continued development. Moreover, graduate students themselves may not have a clear understanding of how the hiring process or governance structures in their department work—though this seems to be changing, with more graduate students coming to understand at least some elements of these structures earlier in their careers.

If the structural elements of faculty work conditions remain largely hidden from graduate students until late in their studies, then students may not have a clear sense of what awaits them if they pursue a faculty career. They may not see their professors' full scope of work—the huge amounts of time devoted to advising and service; the political negotiations that can smooth the road but also take time away from more substantive work; the challenge of maintaining a strong research agenda with numerous competing demands. A recent study by anthropologist John Ziker showed that faculty members typically worked over sixty hours per week, with much of their research time pushed to weekends as meetings and administrative work consumed regular work hours.[22] The freedom to work anywhere and any time can mean that the workday never completely ends. That kind of career doesn't suit everyone, and that's OK. But there's no reason for those realities to remain unknown until someone is seeking a job, or has been hired and is trying to gain their footing in a new department. Graduate students are deeply embedded in their programs, and pulling back the curtain on the realities of faculty careers is something that could be easily incorporated into their intellectual and professional formation.

A more realistic look at the rigors and work styles of a faculty career might make it easier for students to determine whether or not that is a path they wish to pursue. It might result in fewer people taking short-term positions to try to get a foot in the door, only to realize years later that it is rare indeed for a tenure-track hire to be made from among the adjunct ranks. And it might make a shorter path to a more fulfilling career that works for that student's needs.

If faculty work is partially obscured from many students' view, other kinds of intellectual and administrative roles within the university are often even less understood. Students don't always have a chance to see scholarly administrative work up close, even though it facilitates research and teaching, enabling the institution to function. People with PhDs who do find their way into these careers—in administration, educational technology, student affairs, libraries, humanities centers, centers for teaching and learning, and more—often find them deeply fulfilling. In turn, the deep training and familiarity with the structures of higher education that all PhDs gain are an enormous asset in such positions. Moreover, many institutions are developing innovative, cross-disciplinary, and sometimes cross-institutional programs that require a different kind of hybrid faculty/staff employment arrangement. While these kinds of opportunities are sometimes chalked up to administrative bloat, they often involve work that involves generating revenue (read: grantwriting) and that subsequently can create new research opportunities for faculty and students. These can be exciting and intellectually demanding careers, especially for those who want to stay close to the workings of the academy without necessarily pursuing a traditional faculty job. Administrative work can also be appealing for those who want to have an impact not only in their field, but on the structures that govern higher education.

These two trends of increased reliance on adjunct labor and the growth of new, hybrid opportunities throughout university structures are somewhat at odds. Taken together, they suggest that while there is increased risk for what a student's future career path may hold, there is also an increased opportunity for those seeking employment within higher education—but the opportunity may not coincide with graduate students' expectations.

Where Do We Go From Here?

The reliance on adjunct teaching labor has become so extensive that reform can seem daunting. But there are signs of positive change. Thanks in part to baseline recommendations by organizations like the MLA, some faculty unions have successfully pushed for increased per-course compensation rates and longer-term contracts. Increasing public awareness plays an important role in putting pressure on university administrations to work toward greater equity, and on state legislators to increase funding for higher education. But there is a very long way to go, and it can be hard to know where to begin.

Where *Not* to Start: Shrinking Grad Programs across the Board

Balancing the questions of access to graduate education, equity within graduate programs, and fair structures for graduate student labor is a difficult task. One common refrain is that graduate programs should be much smaller so that there is a smaller pool of adjunct labor and less of a supposed "oversupply" of highly educated graduates. But this argument is a misnomer and a distraction. Some graduate programs should indeed be smaller. I firmly believe that programs have an ethical imperative to support the graduate students they admit, both financially, through tuition waivers and some form of compensated work, and intellectually and professionally, through advising and mentorship. When such support is impossible, programs should indeed reduce their numbers until they can offer it to every doctoral student. However, reducing the number of PhDs entering the job market will not balance the system, but rather will contribute to a cycle that devalues humanities education by reinforcing the idea that the only valuable career path is as a faculty member.

There are several reasons why a push to reduce the size of doctoral programs is problematic. First, faculty hiring decisions are not tied to the number of graduating PhDs. The cost-cutting measure of using more and more contingent faculty members can and does operate entirely independently of the number of PhDs on the market. In fact, reducing a graduate program's size can actually perpetuate the increased use of adjuncts, because it may reduce the resources a program receives from the institution, thereby reducing the number of full-time faculty lines available. The reduced funding may prompt programs to meet teaching needs by hiring adjunct faculty on an as-needed basis as undergraduate enrollments continue to rise.[23] Further, the hiring pool is not limited to people with PhDs. According to the 2012 report of the Coalition on the Academic Workforce, 40.2 percent of contingent faculty members hold a master's degree as their highest degree, while 30.4 percent hold a PhD.[24] If the increase in adjunct hiring were directly correlated with an oversupply of PhDs looking for jobs, it would be unlikely that such a high percentage of people with MAs would be hired for such roles. Instead, the numbers show that even now more adjuncts hold MAs than PhDs. This suggests that even if the number of job-seeking PhDs were to decrease, universities would not suddenly find themselves with nobody to teach the necessary courses; hiring would simply shift even more toward people with MAs. A reduction in the number of PhDs available will not significantly change the available labor pool and would not likely result in any major change to hiring practices.[25]

Second, instituting blanket reductions in program size is likely to reinforce conservative decision-making in the admissions process, leading committees to compete over the prospective students with the greatest pedigree and most traditionally legible CV. Measures of selectivity, even if they are thought to be neutral, tend to reward students from wealthy and highly educated families. This means that if graduate programs focus on becoming more selective, the result will likely be a whiter, wealthier student body and a reduction in diversity of all kinds. This in turn will narrow the overall breadth of creativity and vision in new scholarship.

Finally, and more to the point for this book, faculty careers are not the only measure of success for PhD holders. Many different career paths offer satisfying professional trajectories, and encouraging humanities scholars to engage more deeply in other sectors—in and around the academy, as well as in not-for-profits, government, and businesses—would be beneficial to the broader public. As critical pedagogy and educational technology expert Jesse Stommel put it in a blog post, "I want the system to assure my doctor has read all the books of Jane Austen, because critical thinking is what will help them save my life when they encounter a situation they've never encountered before."[26] More varied employment and public engagement can also create a positive feedback loop back into the academy, increasing the importance of publicly relevant research, writing, and teaching.

For all these reasons, trying to reach a one-to-one equilibrium between graduates and tenure-track jobs may be not only counterproductive but also undesirable. Most humanities programs do not need to be stripped down; on the contrary, they need to be made more robust—and that can be a contentious argument to make in a climate of scarcity. Departments need sufficient resources to allow them to invest in full-time employment lines and to provide funding and support for graduate students.

Reducing doctoral programs in response to low tenure-track employment rates strips other environments—whether scholarly, cultural, governmental, nonprofit, or something else entirely—of the advantages that deeply trained humanists can offer. As historian Abby Smith Rumsey has argued, a broad range of opportunities are available to graduates who look beyond the university, where many organizations have a significant need for the skills and approaches that humanists could offer.[27] Humanities programs should not be sacrificed in deference to problematic labor trends; rather, the moment is right to consider the value that humanities education can provide in a broader range of roles that are more deeply engaged with the public, and to encourage students to focus on new ways to engage in public discourse.

Advocacy and Action

Given that both research integrity and teaching outcomes are compromised by poor labor conditions, everyone with a stake in higher education has reason to work to solve the problem. While there is a very long way to go, there has been some movement on overall awareness and advocacy. In 2015, National Adjunct Walkout Day marked an important moment in the effort to raise awareness about faculty labor conditions. The Adjunct Project, mentioned earlier, focused on simply gathering compensation information to try and shed light on how widespread (and how severe) the issue of low wages is across part-time faculty positions. This may seem basic, but because hiring and labor practices are idiosyncratic and are kept highly private, uncovering and sharing factual information is an essential part of bringing about change. The issue of adjunct labor inequality has also risen to public consciousness through the higher education press, mainstream media, and the blogging community with new urgency (recent examples include Carmen Maria Machado writing for the *New Yorker*; Laura McKenna and Caroline Fredrickson for the *Atlantic*; Lee Hall for the *Guardian*; and L. V. Anderson for *Slate*).[28] However, these outlets often struggle to make sense of the disconnect between the rising cost of tuition and the bleak employment circumstances of most faculty.

How can it be that the price tag for a college education keeps inflating, while many contingent faculty members rely on food stamps? There are more factors at play in universities' financial model than simply tuition and faculty wages. As other sources of revenue diminish—especially public tax support and grant funding—schools often rely on tuition dollars to make up the difference. At elite private institutions, the sticker price is sometimes seen as a marker of value, with the suggestion that a higher cost signifies a higher-quality education. Even if the school offers significant financial aid and few people pay that high list price, it has the very real effect of nudging up costs at peer institutions— and may deter some people from even applying. The ready availability of loans is another factor; some schools increase their tuition prices assuming that federal or private loans will make up the difference, resulting in a huge burden of debt for many students.[29] And, finally, student services have increased at many institutions. Central resources like career services, teaching centers, support for women and LGBTQ+ communities, and many other kinds of support are part of what is commonly lumped in with high executive salaries as "administrative bloat" despite being critically important, especially to underserved students.[30] Given this complex financial landscape, it's not enough to push for a single solution at a time without an awareness of how it fits in with the whole. Effective advocacy efforts require a solid understanding of the full picture of labor structures across academic systems so that scholars and students can target our efforts toward the most problematic elements while strengthening the positions that provide genuine professional development and student support.

Another thing that makes activism around contingent labor issues so difficult is that there are so many valences of contingency, some of which are more problematic than others. A postdoc can be a career turning point—in my own experience, a brief eighteen-month stint at the University of Virginia to work with the Scholarly Communication Institute and the Scholars' Lab was transformative. But the position didn't yield a positive experience simply by accident and good fortune; it required careful structuring, mentorship, and opportunities for me to have ownership of certain projects, and to connect me with leaders in the field who would become part of my own network for future growth.[31] All of that takes time and energy on the part of staff and faculty—and they cannot devote that time if they have no stability themselves. Similarly, well-structured graduate teaching positions are invaluable opportunities to learn effective pedagogical approaches before deciding whether one wants to seek a faculty career, provided that they are thoughtfully structured with true opportunities for professional development. There are elements of some short-term, contractual positions that are valuable opportunities for growth; however, the good examples are becoming eclipsed by exploitative short-term or part-time positions, and are sometimes lumped in with them in unhelpful ways.

It's not easy to untangle these threads, and even the seemingly simple task of documenting the number and type of contingent positions is a significant challenge. For instance, as a public institution, the City University of New York publicly shares a great deal of information about its faculty makeup. However, in the public data, CUNY's faculty positions are documented simply as full-time, part-time, or graduate assistantships, which leaves considerable ambiguity. The full-time faculty count includes all tenure-line positions, but also many that are not. The number of part-time faculty members includes people teaching as their main livelihood, as well as graduate students who pick up courses to supplement their fellowships, and professionals who teach as a side gig. Further, the ways in which the different types of positions affect each other are complicated. The City University of New York has reduced the teaching load of most doctoral students on fellowship to one course per semester, which is wonderful. But that reduction in workload also increased CUNY's already heavy reliance on adjuncts who earn an average of $3,275 (as reported by the CUNY Adjunct Project based on data from the Professional Staff Congress, the union for CUNY faculty and staff).[32] Some of these adjuncts include other Graduate Center students who are not receiving fellowship packages, putting them on different footing from their peers. Even when there is progress, gains by one faction of the instructional faculty can come at the expense of another—and almost always, it is adjuncts who lose out.

Renewing the Commitment to Teaching

One possible starting point for reform is a renewed focus on the practice of teaching and the importance of solid pedagogy. The fact that such a high percentage of teaching duties have shifted to adjunct instructors signals an important issue related to values. Teaching, especially at the introductory level, is implicitly seen as something that any qualified person could do in a pinch. Given this tacit assumption, teaching is typically far less valued than research in the RI institutions where most doctoral students are trained. And yet, in community colleges, small liberal arts colleges, and other teaching-focused colleges, pedagogy is taken seriously and excellent teachers are regarded with admiration. How can we bridge the gap between the devaluation of teaching in research-intensive institutions and its high importance at other kinds of institutions?

To say that teaching is fundamental to higher education feels tautological, and yet that value is not always apparent. As Fred Moten and Stefano Harney put it, "It is teaching that brings us in. Before there are grants, research, conferences, books, and journals there is the experience of being taught and of teaching."[33] As a starting point, teaching is also seen as something to move beyond—to reach the more prestigious work of individual scholarly research. With institutional eyes focused on the research prize, many graduate programs never help students move from a love of learning and a passion for a particular subject to an understanding of the craft of teaching, even after spending abundant time in the classroom. Such an approach leaves graduate students ill prepared for faculty careers, especially at teaching-focused institutions. Appropriately valuing and rewarding teaching rather than devaluing it or making it secondary to research is crucial for several reasons. First, graduate students pick up on signals about what matters. If there is no professional development built into their teaching duties, or if they feel that teaching isolates them from colleagues or is seen as a distraction from research, they will understand that it is less valued. If they see that pedagogy is not taken seriously, or that research matters most for tenure, they will adjust their own focus and energy accordingly. They will be primed to perpetuate the subordination of teaching to research.

Second, academic leaders owe it to undergraduate students to better equip graduate students—the next generation of professors, and often the instructor of record in their own right—for the classroom. Today's undergraduate students are increasingly diverse, a bit older, more often from poorer families, and frequently the first in their families to attend college. Are our graduate students ready to teach them? In many ways, community colleges today are doing the lion's share of genuine pedagogical training and the development of creative approaches to the classroom. However, because few graduate students have attended community college, they have experienced neither the challenges of teaching complex material when students are distracted by competing obligations and worries nor the reward of successfully implementing a pedagogical approach that engages students in a new and deep way. If this generation of undergraduates is to succeed academically—to go on to graduate school, to bring their diverse perspectives and experiences and ways of thinking into the structures of the academy—they must be taught well. And graduate students must be prepared to teach them well.

Third, if teaching is undervalued, programs risk losing even more tenure lines to lower-investment adjunct positions. The increasing prevalence of adjuncts is not only bad for adjuncts; it also increases the burden of service duties by distributing them among fewer faculty members, and it erodes the possibility of true shared governance.[34] When tenured faculty members seek course releases or avoid teaching intro-level courses, that sends a signal that the work is undesirable, which sends the signal that no one will mind if it is passed off to graduate students and adjuncts for a much cheaper hourly rate. Rewarding teaching does not just mean adequate compensation, but also genuine attention to the quality of teaching that is formally recognized in the tenure and promotion process. Ideally, quality should be measured through mechanisms other than student evaluations, which are notoriously unreliable and deeply biased, as has been repeatedly demonstrated by multiple studies.[35] Teaching does not need to be a lonely endeavor; departments could structure in much more collegiality and collaboration so that faculty members can learn from one another and feel more connected to their colleagues. Starting this work at the graduate level is essential.

Reinvesting in the craft of excellent teaching and supporting students as they hone their skills is an important component of meaningful career preparation. Far from being at cross-purposes, working toward greater career diversity while also actively pushing for more equitable labor structures are complementary efforts. Together, they constitute a valuable and holistic set of reforms that will do more than improve the outcomes for a small set of borderline cases; rather, they can begin to transform higher education into a more equitable and dynamic system that is both healthier and has stronger public impact.

Inclusive Systems, Vibrant Scholarship

Academic labor structures may be broken, but even so, there has never been a more important moment to embark on the journey of deep humanities study and methodological training. The key is to engage in that scholarly work while also taking steps toward repairing, restoring, and reforming problematic structures—something that both students and faculty can do, albeit in different ways and with different levels of power and risk. In the previous chapter, I considered the challenges of current labor structures and the importance of reinvesting in teaching. In this chapter and the one that follows, I expand that vision to argue that supporting varied career outcomes while also investing in teaching is a crucial way to connect humanities research with the public and, by extension, to support reinvestment in higher education as a public good. I explore this through two different but related avenues that are not often considered in tandem: inclusion and equity in this chapter, and innovative scholarly work in the next.

If doctoral education and scholarly research are to be relevant to public interests, the first step is to ensure that graduate programs are spaces that are genuinely inclusive so that scholarship represents more than a narrow set of perspectives. This is not only a question of "diversity"—a term too easily misused—but also of the rigorous, creative, and broad intellectual inquiry that comes from having students and faculty from a wide range of backgrounds. However, many graduate programs and most university leadership remain overwhelmingly white. Even when institutions make concerted efforts to recruit students and faculty of color, racism and bias within the structures and climate of many departments create environments of hostility. Bringing about greater inclusion in academia—and therefore in scholarly research and teaching—is not a question of numbers or checking boxes, but of the values, culture, and support that enable scholars to thrive. In this chapter, I discuss the stakes of higher education's problems of exclusion and bias, focusing especially on the issue of tacit knowledge and the failure of narrowly defined diversity initiatives. Then, I offer suggestions for fostering greater inclusion, more creative and expansive scholarship, and a stronger sense of public connection. These matters are not tangential to the issue of doctoral education reform, but central.

The topics of inclusivity and innovative research are not often addressed concurrently; instead, so-called diversity initiatives tend to be treated as entirely separate from (and sometimes function at cross-purposes with) programs focused on scholarly communications and public engagement. Reframing both through the lens of the public good helps provide a new orientation that provides a way of understanding the deep connections among varied goals of doctoral education reform: advocating for better policies within the university, supporting a wider range of career outcomes for PhDs, improving student learning, and fostering connections between research institutions and surrounding communities.

What does career preparation have to do with the often disparate matters of inclusion and public engagement? Embracing a wider range of career outcomes and measures of success would mean changing the default institutional mind-set to one in which graduate education is *generative* rather than *reproductive*. This reframing situates reform efforts around career preparation within the much larger project of working toward a more just and equitable system of higher education. While education is one of the pillars that people lean on in order to achieve professional, personal, and financial goals, the challenges of obtaining a degree are rendered even more difficult for people facing bias and discrimination, or for students who may not know how to navigate the structures of academia.

No matter how many diversity initiatives a university launches, true equity will remain out of reach as long as the educational system as a whole continues to ascribe value to deeply conservative processes and outcomes, since the way to measure success will always involve looking back toward those who have come before. While some argue that talking about skills and careers is evidence of neoliberalism at work in the university, it can also be evidence of something quite different. An open and agnostic stance toward outcomes, paired with acceptance of and preparation for a wide range of professional applications, in fact can be a simple but powerful way to work against the inherent conservatism of the university. It is one way of bringing to the fore the realities of life, class, race, bodies, and other sites of lived difference rather than attempting to pursue an idealized, supposedly neutral mode of learning. As bell hooks says in *Teaching to Transgress*, "erasure of the body connects to the erasure of class differences, and more importantly, the erasure of the role of university settings as sites for the reproduction of a privileged class of values, of elitism."[1] Recognizing lived difference is a first step in pushing against the cycle of continued elitism—and allowing space for a wider range of outcomes is one way of recognizing such difference.

Diagnosing the Problem

Education is one of the pillars that people lean on in order to achieve professional, personal, and financial goals. However, the challenges of obtaining a degree are significantly more difficult for people facing bias and discrimination, or for students who may not know how to navigate the structures of academia. At the undergraduate level, recent studies have shown that Black and Latinx students continue to be underrepresented in the academy relative to their share of the US college-aged population—and not only that, but they are in fact underrepresented to a more significant degree now than they were in 1980.[2] Far from being exclusively a student concern, discrimination and bias persist and even worsen at more advanced stages of academic careers. As a result, systemic bias prevents scholars from doing their best work across a wide range of institutions and disciplinary fields.

Despite an abundance of diversity initiatives and pipeline programs designed to recruit students and scholars of color, the proportion of faculty members who identify as racial or ethnic minorities remains incredibly small. More troubling still, the numbers decrease at higher echelons of the academy, as scholars with minority status face uphill battles for tenure and promotion. These challenges are documented in qualitative and quantitative studies as well as in personal narratives that bring emotional and psychological reality to the statistics.

For example, in their annotated bibliography "Gender Bias in Academe," Danica Savonick and Cathy Davidson bring together dozens of studies documenting the ways that women are penalized in the academic workplace.[3] In her edited volume *Written/Unwritten: Diversity and the Hidden Truths of Tenure*, Patricia Matthew offers case studies of some of the obstacles that women of color face in academe—including unclear and variable standards, lack of mentorship, disrespect for a person's scholarship, and veiled or open hostility from colleagues.[4] Similarly, *Presumed Incompetent: The Intersections of Race and Class for Women in Academia* (edited by Gabriella Gutiérrez y Muhs, Yolanda Flores Niemann, Carmen G. González, and Angela P. Harris) uses personal essays to consider the tension between the perceived elitism of a career in higher education and the deeply entrenched biases that people face along gender, race, and class lines.[5] Sara Ahmed's *On Being Included: Racism and Diversity in Institutional Life* offers in-depth considerations of the experiences of faculty members of color and the failure of diversity initiatives, which I will discuss in a moment.[6] These and other works repeatedly demonstrate the ways in which tacit rules and unspoken norms actively harm women-identified scholars of all races and ethnicities, and scholars of color of all genders, who face bias in everything from student evaluations to tenure review. The result may be dramatic and concrete—a denied tenure case, for instance—or the challenges may accumulate slowly, wearing someone down until they eventually step away from a role and an environment that asks the impossible.

Working against higher education's systemic racism and sexism is a matter of fundamental equity, especially since access to quality higher education plays a key role in material and professional success. This connection is apparent even at the undergraduate level: in the United States, people who attain a bachelor's degree have stronger employment prospects and can expect higher salaries than their peers with a high-school diploma. In 2016, the unemployment rate for bachelor's degree holders was 2.7 percent, compared to a national average of 4 percent. Median wages for bachelor's degree holders were about $60,000, compared to $46,000 for those with a high school diploma.[7] The trend continues for those who earn a graduate degree; the unemployment rate for doctoral degree holders was just 1.6 percent, with median earnings of about $86,500. While job hunting is undeniably a difficult endeavor, the numbers show that pursuing advanced degrees does tend to pay off, literally. However, as is true with many systems in the United States that purport to level the playing field, a strong educational foundation is not equally available to all.

While universities foster the development of new knowledge on one hand, they also serve as institutional gatekeepers, determining who can advance, often by applying the same criteria that have been in place for generations. As a result, the students most likely to succeed at every level—to obtain a diploma, to be accepted into graduate school, and to earn a doctoral degree—are those who have been groomed toward that path throughout their lives. What this means in practical terms is that affluent white students with highly educated parents are much more likely to understand and successfully navigate the tacit rules of the academy, and as a result, people of color and people from lower-income families are less likely to advance through graduate school and into senior faculty positions—a phenomenon sometimes described as the "leaky pipeline," especially in reference to women in STEM fields. But a pipeline may be the wrong metaphor, especially if the goal is not simply to reproduce existing structures, but rather to creatively apply research and teaching to a range of contexts. The problem is that the current academic system is structured to reward pipeline thinking—steady advancement through predictable stages.

The notion of a pipeline or predetermined pathway can also apply to the more personal matter of family dynamics and expectations. People whose parents obtained advanced degrees are more likely to pursue graduate work themselves. Since the ability to attend graduate school requires a college degree, it also requires strong K–12 education, which correlates to zip code and family wealth or income. Taken together, these factors perpetuate educational inequity across generations. Data collected in 2015 as part of the Survey of Earned Doctorates reveals that increasingly, people who receive PhDs tend to have parents that are better educated than in earlier cohorts.[8] While this could be due to overall increasing education levels among the US population, it also suggests that fewer first-generation college students are rising through the higher education system to achieve a doctoral degree than in years past. Additional data shows that students from underrepresented groups are more likely than white or Asian students to be the first in their families to attend college, let alone pursue graduate work. These first-generation college students were less likely to receive their degrees from R1 institutions, which would subsequently make them less likely to be hired as faculty members at research-intensive institutions. First-generation students also tended to have higher levels of debt and longer time-to-degree (an average of ten years or longer in the humanities and education) than their peers who were second-generation students or later. Taken together, these data points suggest that the decreasing share of first-generation college students among PhD recipients may also have a negative effect on racial and ethnic diversity, not only among a single cohort of graduate students, but for generations of academic study.

When I conducted the "Humanities Unbound" study in 2012, I moved around matters of identity with great caution. Questions about respondents' self-identified race, ethnicity, gender, and caregiver status appeared at the end of the survey, and while most data was publicly available, demographic data was held in a restricted database requiring research justification prior to access. More than anything, the results revealed the need for further study on matters of identity and life outside of work (whether one cares for a child, an aging parent, or other family member, for instance), given that these could be deciding factors that lead someone to seek a particular type of employment, or that determine the opportunities that may be available to them. I received resistance from some respondents who maintained that race, ethnicity, and gender were irrelevant—or even that such questions were offensive. And yet this resistance itself may be evidence of the importance of better understanding the individual and systemic factors and patterns that make some paths more appealing than others to people in historically marginalized positions in the academy. Refusing to examine the relationships between identity and experience in academic or other professional pathways is likely to reinscribe existing structures of power and privilege.

The reality is that many nonprofessional factors—related to identity, family commitments, health, and more—have a significant bearing on a person's career. These factors must be part of the equation to fully understand whether a professional environment is supportive and inclusive. In particular, the reasons people in historically marginalized groups may opt out (or be nudged out) of the professoriate reflect systemic bias as well as personal choice—and the result is significant. Even with universities trying to implement more diverse hiring practices, the percentage of women and people of color tends to decrease at higher faculty ranks.[9] In 2015, only 23 percent of all faculty members nationwide identified as belonging to a racial or ethnic category other than white. At the level of full professor, that number decreases to 18 percent.[10] Scholars from historically marginalized groups are underrepresented across all levels of academic programs, from graduate students to faculty, but constitute a vanishingly small proportion of faculty at the most senior levels of the profession. In other words, the problem is not only one of recruitment, but also of retention, suggesting that workplace climate and advancement practices are partly to blame. This lack of diversity among faculty members negatively affects all students, impacting learning outcomes and overall student experience.[11] When the workplace culture of universities is not truly inclusive, faculty members of color face an uphill battle for professional recognition and full, respected participation in their departments. Such an environment also perpetuates a value system that implicitly rewards conformity and deprives students of a much more comprehensive education that would include a wider range of voices and perspectives, and many different kinds of knowledge.

Lack of diversity, especially among senior faculty, is an issue across all academic disciplines. Research in the biomedical field, for instance, has shown that while diversity is increasing in graduate programs in that field, there has been a much smaller relative increase among faculty.[12] In addition to the very real factors of bias and discrimination, another element contributing to the discrepancy may be that for some, other opportunities are simply more appealing. While the specific factors involved will certainly vary across fields, there is likely both a push (out of academia) and a pull (into other professional domains) on many students who do not feel at home in academia. The push comes in part from microaggressions, bias, and the countless ways that underrepresented minorities are made to feel "other" and unwelcome (even though such hostilities unfortunately exist in many nonacademic contexts as well). The pull may come from material factors such as salary, benefits, and the geographic location of other job opportunities, as well as intangible but vitally important questions of meaning, mission, and impact.

Looking at gender as an example, about half of all college and university faculty members are women, but they tend to be concentrated among the lower ranks or in contingent positions, or both.[13] Women also tend to be overrepresented among non-tenure-track faculty members in most humanities disciplines,[14] and the gender wage gap is higher among humanities PhDs than in any other field (besides business), with median earnings of $95,000 for men compared to just $63,000 for women.[15] And yet, outside of faculty positions, current estimates indicate that about 64 percent of education administrators are women.[16] Taken together, these numbers suggest that women are not being sufficiently rewarded in faculty careers, and are opting into administrative roles.

I suspect that for women who transition into academic administration, the decision has to do not only with professional goals and aptitudes, but also biased workplace structures and gender norms related to caregiving responsibilities. It is still typically women who take on the role of primary caregiver, and it has been documented that women face a wage penalty when they have children, whereas men do not.[17] Faculty careers often require years of precarious positions and frequent uprooting, and even at their best may bleed into all hours of the day and night (one of the pitfalls of a seemingly flexible schedule)—factors that may be unappealing or untenable when one is also the primary caregiver for kids or other family members. Even in a stable, tenure-track role, the tenure process itself is extremely difficult to manage for women who hope to start a family, or who are already caregivers. As a result, some women opt out of the tenure stream before even attempting it, seeing the difficult choices that it forces upon their mentors and peers. Instead, women often take on part-time roles as adjuncts, or seek positions that offer hours more consistent with standard daycare centers. (As someone with two young kids of my own, I can say that having a position that makes it possible for me to leave in time to pick up my kids at daycare—and that leaves my weekends mostly free—has been essential.) Yet the other roles that women take on are not often recognized or held up as models. Recalibrating norms and definitions of success would mean that all of these cases would be celebrated, rather than rendered invisible. However, focusing on gender in isolation is an incomplete view, one that privileges white cisgender women without doing enough to support equity for all. For women of color or others whose identities reflect the intersection of multiple axes of bias,[18] reform within graduate programs is only a small component of the much broader renewal that is needed throughout not only the education sector, but dominant economic and social structures in the United States as a whole.

All of these factors, as well as the bias, microaggressions, and hurdles that minority scholars face in graduate school and as faculty members, serve to centralize and normalize whiteness at an institutional level. As Patricia Matthew notes, "We still need to figure out the ways in which the academy is structurally hostile to diversity and how to unpack the unwritten codes . . . that make it difficult for faculty of color to succeed."[19] Far from being a matter of perception, bias against scholars of color who are women is visible in the rather shocking percentages of successful (and unsuccessful) tenure cases at various institutions that Matthew cites in her introduction. At the University of Southern California, the percentage of white men in the humanities and social sciences who were awarded tenure between 1998 and 2012 was 92 percent. For women and faculty of color, that number was 55 percent, and for faculty of color alone, the number was 48 percent.[20] This is not a blip: the numbers evidence a prolonged and systemic reality; USC is far from the only place where this is true, and, indeed, it is rare for this data to even be made available.

Tacit Knowledge and the Illusion of Merit

Advising and mentorship, whether formal or informal, is an essential factor in student success at both the undergraduate and graduate level. For many, especially for first-generation college students, a mentor may be the first person to urge a student to consider graduate school and convince them that they "belong" in an academic environment. This was certainly true for me; though my parents both have college educations, graduate school was not something that was on my radar until two faculty members at my undergraduate institution, professors Nestor Quiroa and David Wright, separately encouraged me to think about applying to PhD programs and advised me on my options. (I will be forever grateful to them not only for believing in my potential but also for strongly urging me to pursue an option that would not leave me mired in student loans.)

Once I was immersed in my doctoral program at the University of Colorado, my dissertation advisor, Warren Motte, not only helped me move through the exam and dissertation stages with minimal anguish, but also pulled back the curtain on the mysteries of scholarly publishing, job opportunities, and more— while fully respecting the ways in which my goals differed from his own path.

In retrospect, I have been surprised and somewhat aggrieved to reflect on how few of my early academic mentors were women. The professional mentors who have had the most significant impact on me later in my trajectory have nearly all been women, and I wonder why I didn't connect more deeply with the women faculty members with whom I worked as a student, or how my path might have been different if I had. Matters of identity may seem incidental, but they are often deeply important to the mentoring relationship, especially for people who identify with a group that is underrepresented in their field or in the academy more broadly. This is one of the reasons that women and minority faculty members often have a much heavier service and advising load than their white male peers; students frequently gravitate toward faculty members who they feel will hear and understand them.

And, yet, most graduate programs leave first-generation and minority students to sink or swim. This is especially unfortunate given that the tacit knowledge that can make or break a student's success is not at all indicative of their ability to research, think, analyze, write, or perform any of the other core tasks of doctoral study—and yet they can utterly derail a student's progress. Education scholars Dorian McCoy and Rachelle Winkle-Wagner describe the ways that understanding oneself as a scholar, and as belonging in a scholarly environment, is often essential for incoming graduate students from marginalized groups. They suggest that the converse, a lack of connection and socialization, may negatively affect a student's sense of belonging within a program, the kinds of opportunities that are offered to her during her program, and her likelihood to complete the degree. For instance, they describe the value of summer "bridge" programs in helping students to internalize this new aspect of their identity: "A two-way scholarly habitus development suggests the participants now considered themselves scholars, even though some of them had previously admitted they thought there was no space in academia for people with their identities."[21] Seeing oneself as simply belonging in academic space is an essential step toward succeeding in that environment. The early stages of graduate school are often replete with tacit knowledge, leaving those who are less familiar with academic structures and processes to flounder despite their best efforts. Though community college and undergraduate populations are more diverse than ever, in 2015 only 10.5 percent of humanities doctoral degrees were conferred to members of what Humanities Indicators terms "traditionally under-represented racial/ethnic groups."[22] This disparity is often worse in the humanities than in STEM fields.[23] Just like first-generation undergraduate students, graduate students who are the first in their families to work toward a PhD face a steep challenge in their studies to master not only their subject area, but the systems of which they are a part.

An understanding of the cultural codes and unspoken rules of academia is often conflated with merit or achievement—even brilliance, as Julie Posselt notes.[24] But academic cultural capital is not aptitude—it is merely an understanding of the systems and processes that govern academia and an ability to navigate them. As Lani Guinier explores in *The Tyranny of the Meritocracy*, the consistent allegiance to "merit" as a concept despite a changing and problematic definition (one that currently rewards existing privilege over other factors) results in a system that perpetuates bias but perceives itself as fair and equal.[25] Guinier makes it clear that what is often called "merit" is actually deeply linked with whiteness. Until that connection is examined and disentangled, diversity initiatives will, at most, serve to inject more people from underrepresented groups into an environment that continues to value attributes that are markers of privilege more than anything else.

This question of values is fundamental to the entire academic enterprise—how we understand matters of admissions, retention, degree conferral, entrance into faculty careers, and tenure and promotion. Who has access to and succeeds in the world of higher education often hinges on matters that are too often implicit and opaque, shrouded in vague terms like "merit" and "fit." Terms like these, used by admissions committees and hiring committees to signal who is and is not poised to succeed in the academy, often mask conservative tendencies that seek to preserve the status quo—which is one of deep-seated inequality rooted in racism and sexism. Such tendencies maintain the dominant (white, male) power structures of the academy, depriving classrooms of the knowledge and perspectives of prospective future faculty, and deepening inequality at a moment when educational success is paramount for professional success.

The Failure of Diversity Initiatives

It may seem that universities can improve diversity and inclusion simply by recruiting more students and faculty of color, but time and again initiatives that aim to do so prove inadequate. As Sara Ahmed describes in *On Being Included*, efforts to increase "diversity" within universities may do worse than fall flat—they may in fact serve to reinscribe and solidify whiteness as the default.[26] By many measures, these initiatives are failing. While raw numbers of underrepresented minority students and faculty may be increasing somewhat, the gains are mostly modest and often belie the difficulties and bias that women and people who present as women, people of color, LGBTQ+ people, and people with disabilities continue to face in academic environments.

Ahmed's research helps make sense of why this is the case. Rather than giving those who lead diversity efforts sufficient authority to actually change things, diversity initiatives often result in nothing more than a document that outlines either goals or process or both. The existence of the document is taken by the university to mean that they are "good" at diversity and their work is therefore done, whereas in reality the necessity of such a document underscores the opposite—that whiteness is the norm and diversity remains an additive. But with the document in hand, it becomes easier for the university to *not* act, because in the institutional mind, the action has already occurred. Another common approach, one that purports to be "colorblind" and purely meritocratic, is equally problematic and ignores the real ways that race and other identity categories have real impact on people's lived experiences, for instance through housing inequities and predatory lending practices that have made it difficult or impossible for many families of color to build wealth and stability across generations.[27] The resulting underrepresentation does a disservice to all students and impoverishes academic discourse.

It would seem that a genuine thirst for new knowledge and creative lines of inquiry would lead universities to examine the systems that limit the success of underrepresented students, and yet white faculty and administrators continue to lament a lack of diversity on one hand while failing to examine the incentives and structures that reward conservatism. Given this dispiriting reality, it is no wonder that diversity initiatives may have paltry results at best; even if they are created with the best of intentions (which they sometimes are—though not always), such initiatives attempt to bring underrepresented scholars into an institutional setting that does not support them and without real change happening at the level of the institution itself.

If diversity initiatives do not create an inclusive space for teaching, learning, and research, then what can be done? I do not claim to have answers to this question that many have worked on for generations (often running into the "brick wall" that Ahmed both describes and visually represents in her work). What is clear is that people in positions of power and stability must go deeper and be less self-satisfied with results that merely reassert the dominance of already-dominant groups. Truly inclusive practices are not merely a matter of recruitment, but rather require a long and patient consideration of the fundamental values that perpetuate inequality in higher education. Part of this effort involves redefining what is meant by "success" in an academic context, and how that success can be evaluated, rewarded, and shared.

Building an Inclusive Professoriate

Establishing an inclusive, equitable environment in which a broader range of scholars thrive, then, requires far more than one-off diversity initiatives. Rather than attempting to bring more scholars of color into an environment that is stacked against their success, faculty and administrators wishing to make a change must examine the ways in which the structures of the academy reproduce the conditions that privilege whiteness and maleness. Efforts that may lead to long-term change include understanding students' motivations and values; changing admissions practices; building support networks; and rethinking definitions of knowledge production and scholarly success (which I will explore in depth in the next chapter).

Understand Student Motivations and Values

To make a significant change requires understanding the individual and structural factors surrounding gender, race, ethnicity, and sexual orientation that affect students' academic trajectories. Elements of students' family and home lives may prompt them either to consider or reject the prospect of graduate study for a range of reasons. As an example, education scholars Karen J. Haley, Audrey J. Jaeger, and John S. Levin found a stronger connection between parental involvement with eventual career choice among undergraduate students of color than among white students.[28] In their research, students of color often cited making career choices based on ways they thought they could best support their family (monetarily, through proximity and availability, or in other ways), which often led them away from humanities fields or the pursuit of research degrees. Other goals included balance, community engagement, and an identity as a role model. Doctoral education does not need to function at cross-purposes with familial commitments and motivations, but it often does; indeed, these goals were sometimes considered incompatible with faculty positions. Deeper opportunities for public engagement paired with a celebration of the many possible outcomes that follow graduate training may help alleviate the dissonance that students perceive.

At the same time, celebrating the pathways of those who choose varied career paths cannot be the only strategy. Universities must also become more serious about fighting gender bias and creating inclusive and supportive policies that enable women to do their best work. Policy changes including rethinking classroom evaluations, fostering greater transparency in the tenure and promotion process, offering improved family leave and childcare policies, and more are all essential elements of building a healthier and more inclusive discipline. A feminist approach to doctoral education and career preparation, then, would recognize gender-based bias; the biological and social realities of gestation, lactation, and childcare for those who have children; the priorities and skills that are undervalued because they are coded feminine, and more. A frank recognition of the factors that both empower and hinder women from achieving full and meaningful participation in all levels of the academy would help release graduate students of all genders from the pressure to conform to a particular path, and would enable them to more freely pursue opportunities that are meaningful to them and that build on their strengths and interests.

Graduate programs are losing excellent prospective students and the knowledge and experience they bring for many reasons that connect—directly or indirectly—to students' perception that grad school leads primarily to faculty careers. First, underrepresented and first-generation students may have important career goals that they perceive as being at odds with a possible faculty career, such as taking care of family, which would necessitate geographic proximity and adequate compensation. Second, students from modest family backgrounds may consider the time required to complete a PhD—an average of nine years in the humanities according to the Survey of Earned Doctorates— an unacceptably long time to be out of the workforce, both in terms of income as well as potential advancement. Particularly for students of color and first-generation students, this fact in itself may be a deterrent from pursuing a graduate degree. Finally, students may examine the demographic makeup of most research faculties and find few people with backgrounds similar to theirs, leading them to conclude that they will find limited opportunity in the profession.

Change Admissions Practices

Of course, a person cannot thrive in a program unless they enter it in the first place. The graduate admissions process is a potentially transformative and often unexamined element of reform. The process plays a significant role in not only the obvious question of *who* participates in a doctoral program but also in the resulting dynamics of that program. It is also a mirror showing how a program understands itself and its values. The process of deciding on each new cohort tends to reinforce existing power structures, as Julie R. Posselt demonstrates in *Inside Graduate Admissions.*[29] In her research, she found not only that the criteria that admissions committees used were likely to favor applicants with identities that aligned with the existing departmental majority, but also the structures of committees themselves—often lacking gender, racial, or ethnic diversity. Moreover, the processes that many committees used minimized the possibility of truly democratic decisions by focusing on efficiency rather than hearing all voices, something deemed necessary by the high number of applicants and the labor-intensive nature of the admissions committee work.

The admissions process is the first of many evaluative processes by which faculty assess the work of their potential future colleagues and, in determining what is acceptable and desirable, reinforce the definitions and boundaries of what they consider the merit of their own work to be. It is both a rigorous and a self-referential process. Each selection solidifies what kinds of outcomes will be expected not only from an incoming cohort, but from future cohorts as well, since newer students often look to those further in their studies for cues about expectations. As Posselt notes, "Selecting students was therefore not only about *predicting* who would be successful in the future. It was about *creating* their programs' futures by selecting new members who would uphold the core, identity, and status of the group."[30] Selecting people who will succeed differently is the first step to establishing new measures of value, but once again, this is not an isolated matter; it is deeply connected with other structures and values in the academy.

To date, the university has been a largely conservative system that values new insights and scholarship, but only through the mechanism of reproducing the same structures generation after generation. Kandice Chuh, American studies professor and past president of the American Studies Association, describes the process as a fantasy: "If we pay attention to the ways that our own attachments condition the selection not of a student but instead of a particular fantasy of the good life, the ways in which the ordinary practices of the university (re)produce the privileging, the mattering, of some attachments over others come into relief."[31] Faculty members know their fields extremely well and are trained to sense who is likely to succeed in joining their ranks—when success is measured by past success. They are likely less versed, however, in evaluating prospective students for other kinds of scholarly and social contributions that may look radically different than what has come before.

As long as graduate school is seen as preparation for the student to take on the role of the professor, it makes sense that programs and individual faculty members would continue to seek, accept, train, and value students who demonstrate similar strengths and aptitudes held by the professors themselves. As an example, admissions committee evaluators interviewed by Posselt noted that traits like curiosity, creativity, and passion were appealing characteristics in prospective students. However, by prescreening the pool for traditional markers of "merit" before evaluating materials more fully, they likely eliminated applicants who could bring the greatest innovation to their programs without giving their applications full consideration.[32] By the same token, breaking free of the mind-set of apprenticeship and allowing a greater degree of uncertainty in terms of what constitutes success may help open the doors of graduate programs to students with different backgrounds, strengths, and goals.

Admissions processes could be assessing whether students show community involvement, passion for social justice, an aptitude and curiosity for learning the latest technology, an ability to express their thoughts in a way that reaches people beyond the academy. Perhaps admissions committees could bring in outside evaluators to contribute to the selection process, much in the way that funders share grant proposals with outside reviewers with different areas of expertise. Such a connection could even be one component of a deep partnership with a local community organization. The program might invite leaders from that organization to have a voice on committees, while also giving back to the organization by embedding students in project-based roles related to their areas of research. Such a partnership would need to be carefully crafted and maintained to ensure that both parties felt nourished by the relationship, but at its best it could bring a new immediacy, grounding, and vibrancy to a PhD program.

Increasing representation in graduate programs is a necessary step, not only to improve the health and vibrancy of graduate programs but also to ensure equal opportunities to varied employment outcomes.[33] Unfortunately, the admissions process too often replicates existing inequalities, with diversity only factoring into decisions for select edge cases. For instance, Graduate Record Examination (GRE) scores remain a key primary indicator and initial sorting mechanism for many admissions committees, despite the demonstrated inequality inherent in standardized testing. Even when later rounds of applicant evaluation are more holistic, many prospective students from diverse backgrounds are eliminated before ever reaching that stage. Committees may think that quantitative measures such as the GRE are objective; however, if those measures are not critically examined, the process itself remains highly subjective.

Actively working against implicit bias in the admissions process is a key step to fostering more broadly representative cohorts that include students who are not only committed to academic excellence but also to a wider range of engagements such as community involvement, family duties, artistic expression, political activism, and more. This breadth naturally lends itself to greater breadth in career pathways, since students enter the program with different goals that shape their scholarly and professional trajectories.

Build Support Networks

The importance of strong mentoring relationships is clear, particularly for students less familiar with the US higher education system. The reality, though, is that good mentoring is difficult and often invisible work, and is not typically professionally valued in the same way that publishing or teaching are. The workload is often greatest for faculty members who are women and people of color. Because mentoring happens in one-on-one circumstances, often with expectations of confidentiality, it is difficult to assess outstanding work of this nature, and it is almost impossible to capture in a tenure file. Given the high stakes, it is crucial to find better mechanisms to make the work of mentorship more visible and professionally valued.

One approach to ascribing higher professional value to mentoring is through carefully structured programs. CUNY's Pipeline Program is an example of a program that leverages the importance of strong personal contact in mentoring and advising relationships in order to help students enter and succeed in graduate school. Offering mentoring as well as financial support, the Pipeline Program combines a six-week intensive research preparation program with monthly colloquia and peer mentoring sessions. The direct, sustained, and personal contact with students is essential to their success. It pairs the teaching of specific skills, such as research and writing, with helping students to recognize that they belong—and can succeed—in a graduate program. By establishing meaningful mentoring and advising relationships not as something that students must seek out on their own, but rather as something that is structurally a part of their program, the uneven foundation of family educational background is minimized as all students have access to the kind of important extracurricular discussions that can sometimes be the difference between applying to grad school or not. By breaking down social, educational, and financial barriers, programs like this work to increase the number of underrepresented minority students who pursue advanced degrees and go on to teach, conduct research, and apply their knowledge.

Peer mentoring can also be a valuable support structure, both for students and for faculty. As Kandice Chuh has noted, traditional mentoring structures can reinforce hierarchies, sometimes in an unhelpful way. Peer mentoring, by contrast, establishes horizontal leadership structures that enable students to see themselves in multiple roles at once—both as someone who is learning and as someone who can teach others. Being able to embrace both roles is an important skill for any profession. It also counters the tendency toward imposter syndrome that is so prevalent in academic circles, because it allows space for everyone to be an expert in some ways and a novice in others, without undermining the areas of expertise. It can create a combination of confidence and humility that makes it far easier to share what one knows without being afraid to admit that there is still much to learn.

At its simplest, peer mentorship can take place through supportive communities, whether in person or virtual. Social media offers informal opportunities for mentorship that can be extremely valuable, especially for students who may feel alone, isolated, or unsupported in their programs. Such spaces can be especially important for first-generation and underrepresented minority students who may have few peers in their programs who can relate to their experiences. The Council of Graduate Schools also found peer mentoring to be an effective tool to support retention and completion among underrepresented minority students in doctoral programs.[34] Describing her experience as a master of fine arts student and woman of color, writer Morgan Jerkins found that Twitter offered support that was unmatched in the predominantly white spaces of many high-prestige, brick-and-mortar institutions: "In academia, we must search for community. On Twitter, it's already waiting for us" (Jerkins 2015).[35] By embracing the possibility afforded by social media to connect across institutions, students can go from being (or feeling like) the only person of color in the room to connecting with many others who share their experience.

One informal effort to counter the effects of differing backgrounds was launched in 2015 by Aimée Morrison, professor of English language and literature at the University of Waterloo. Using the vehicles of a group blog and Twitter, Morrison challenged her peers to share key information that made a difference for their success at the hashtag #tacitphd—information that comes naturally to students who have long been surrounded by the trappings of academe, but is painstakingly difficult to discover for first-generation students or others less familiar with academic environments. As Morrison described in her blog post launching the #tacitphd hashtag, "This stuff can tank people. The hidden curriculum—networking, professional communication, how to spend each day, which tasks and relationships to prioritize, and how—supports the overt one. Tacit knowledge greases the wheels, and in its absence, the wheels grind and spark and fail. . . . For me, [making tacit knowledge explicit] is an equity seeking gesture."[36] Morrison invited others to share their insights; the hundreds of resulting tweets sharing tips on teaching, writing, social norms, work-life balance, and more were then gathered in a Storify by Jennifer Polk, creating an incredibly useful compendium of knowledge that can help students navigate the world of graduate school more fluidly.[37]

Social networks don't eliminate the need for working toward more inclusive institutions—and they can be a site of gendered and racialized violence, with women, especially women of color, finding themselves the targets of threats and doxxing. It is crucial that university administrators think proactively about how to protect and support faculty and graduate students who are subject to online harassment.[38] Still, despite the risks, social networks can fill an important gap until brick-and-mortar institutions catch up. Having such community can be the difference between finishing a dissertation and throwing in the towel.

As a cluster of disciplines, the humanities face a difficult tension in the effort to work against bias and inequity. On one hand, activist scholarship movements in gender studies, racial and ethnic studies, area studies, and more provide humanities scholars with ample context for the history of oppression and marginalization that can and should inform institutional practices. On the other hand, humanities scholarship is subjective by nature and evaluated largely on a basis of reputation and prestige (based on a scholar's institution, a journal or press where their work is published, their networks of citation and influence, and so on), which makes the field highly susceptible to unconscious bias.[39] Indeed, statistics related to hiring and advancement of women and people of color in the humanities are no better than in other disciplines. Lasting change requires going beyond recruitment initiatives and supporting ongoing, active work that ensures that faculty members who are women, people of color, LGBTQ+, and people with disabilities can work in a supportive and growth-oriented environment that values their scholarship and recognizes the historical and contemporary hurdles that hinder them from doing their best work.

Expanding Definitions
of Scholarly Success

The question of what is considered successful in terms of research or career outcomes is at once highly subjective and highly normative, as junior scholars look to more established faculty members for cues about what matters in higher education's prestige economy. In the previous chapter, I discussed the importance of developing inclusive educational structures for the sake of equity, creative research, and the public good. In this chapter, I will build on that thread by considering ways that rethinking widely held practices and common standards for scholarly communication is part of the equation of reestablishing higher education as a public good as well as fostering innovative scholarship. Examining and broadening the definitions of scholarly success creates openings for scholars to expand the impact of their work and spark renewed public interest in research and higher education. Adopting greater flexibility and expansiveness in the definitions of scholarly success, including placing a high value on work that has a significant public impact, is an important element of developing more inclusive academic structures and practices—and may reduce the perceived divide between universities and the broader public. Faculty and students alike can play an important role in opening up their programs to new possibilities.

As state and federal funding for the humanities continues to shrink, the need to share relevant academic thinking outside the university grows ever more important. In today's political rhetoric, higher education has come to be seen as the domain of the elite, antithetical to a swell in populist sentiment. And yet more than 70 percent of all postsecondary students today are enrolled in public colleges and universities, institutions whose missions have historically been deeply grounded in service to the public good.[1] The perceived isolation of the university has contributed to a nationwide mistrust of knowledge and expertise, with a growing sense that the deeper a person dives into specialized knowledge, the further removed they become from the realities of everyday Americans. As a result, public funding for higher education is drying up. As just one example, consider Colorado, where state funding for higher education dropped by 48 percent between 2002 and 2010.[2] At present, funding from the state constitutes only 4.3 percent of the University of Colorado's budget. This lack of funding is evidence that legislators—and the constituents they represent—do not consider their state's public universities worthy of significant investment.

With less state funding, public universities are rapidly becoming unaffordable, making a college education harder for people from poor and working-class backgrounds to obtain, further deepening these divides. Minimal funding also means that faculty and administrators tend to be spread thin, and unpredictable budgets make it extremely difficult to plan truly sustainable, long-term projects. Decreased funding and negative public opinion become a vicious cycle, with each feeding the other until the elitism that was feared becomes reality in a self-fulfilling prophecy, with only the wealthy able to afford an advanced degree. Universities can break this cycle by recommitting to serving the public, both by developing a more fully inclusive professoriate, as discussed in chapter 2, and by fostering creative and publicly engaged research.

Public Support Requires Public Scholarship

The lack of public support for higher education is exacerbated when scholarship does not have a public impact. By current standards in many academic departments, creative ideas for the production of new knowledge, the dissemination of research, and engaged teaching and learning are often met with skepticism and reluctance rather than enthusiasm and encouragement. The formats and platforms that scholars use to share research should be fluid, changing shape to best showcase the new insights they contain. As digital innovation, design, and humanistic inquiry blend in new and unexpected ways, a healthy discipline would recognize the value of such creative work and find new ways to evaluate it. Scholars often feel they must provide a separate piece of work that renders their creative research product in standard scholarly terms—the peer-reviewed article, the monograph—which hampers their ability to do their best and most insightful work. Rather, a discipline that sees and understands its place in the world and that values the impact and reach of its most brilliant scholars would work to eliminate barriers to excellent scholarship and teaching. It is perhaps a failure of the imagination that renders the overwhelming majority of humanities research in formats that the public will never see.

Scholars who take a translational approach, connecting their research with big societal questions or other matters of public interest, help demystify scholarly work and offer a glimpse into the tools of humanistic research and analysis like close reading or archival research. Whether conducting cultural and historical research about a particular neighborhood, advising on ethical considerations of self-driving cars or other emerging technologies, or contextualizing the political landscape, humanities practitioners have crucial roles to play across many sectors. Making that work more visible (and rewarding it professionally) may lead to more porous boundaries between the academy and the broader society, which has the potential to reinvigorate humanities disciplines, spark new and meaningful interdisciplinary research in response to complex problems, and build greater esteem for scholarly work in the public eye. Considering the 2016 dismantling of tenure in Wisconsin, especially with several other states headed down the same road, it is essential that we actively make the case for graduate study not only for the sake of students, but for society.

Ascribing value to public engagement is an important element in shifting the norms around scholarly work. The ability to articulate why public engagement matters is an important component of this—not just as something flashy to add gloss to a CV, but as a substantive and strategic element of meaningful scholarly discourse. Too often, public engagement by scholars is seen as shallow or a mere novelty. As an example, Julie Posselt describes admissions committee conversations in which a prospective student's demonstrated public engagement (writing for *Slate*) was described by an admissions committee member as "cool" rather than in any scholarly terms.[3] The committee member is trying to say something favorable, but it is empty in terms of the values traditionally held by the academy, like rigor, brilliance, originality, or complexity. Writing for *Slate* is absolutely noteworthy, but describing it in this way does a disservice to the prospective student and to the importance of public engagement more broadly. What matters about writing for mainstream publications is the ability to translate work for a nonspecialist audience in a way that is compelling. That is huge, and relatively uncommon among scholars.

People working on projects with high potential impact may not be served by focusing on writing a peer-reviewed journal article; instead, their scholarship may be best communicated through policy briefs, public talks, digital projects, or many other formats. In an ideal world, this could become a virtuous circle—

graduate programs recruit and admit students with interest in articulating and applying their research to the world in creative ways; faculty members support that process and perhaps envision new possibilities for their own research; programs and institutions recognize and reward the value of that work. It begins to grow easier to recruit and retain not only students but also faculty who seek to make new kinds of connections with their research. As measures of success become more expansive, the conservative nature of the university is loosened, and the institution slowly moves away from valorizing a particular kind of knowledge that is also bound up with whiteness and elitism.

If humanities programs were to emphasize this potential for connection, gainful employment, and meaningful applicability, it would represent a significant stride in reasserting higher education as a public good rather than a private and elite undertaking. Shifting from the perception of university as ivory tower to the university as public commons requires a high degree of crossover between formal educational spaces and surrounding communities. An ivory tower connotes an inward-looking profession—one that shields itself from the noise of the outside world and as a result is difficult to access. It can also be a mechanism of surveillance and defense, offering a high vantage point that can see all but is inaccessible to all but a select few.[4] A commons, by contrast, is loud, messy, and open; it suggests a cacophony of voices and wide range of influences. It is easy to enter and easy to leave, and is an integral space for the community. The latter image of the university suggests a far more inclusive space, with many more people invested in the activities that happen there. There is also a greater likelihood of surprising or unexpected outcomes than in the university as ivory tower. While the university-as-commons is much more likely to yield systems and scholarship that support the public good, the conservatism inherent in universities makes it difficult to foster such radical openness.

There is evidence that the public desires greater access to high-level research and teaching, particularly when it is disentangled from formal (and costly) institutions. Consider, for instance, the Brooklyn Institute for Social Research (BISR). Founded in 2012 by Abby Kluchin and Ajay Chaudhary, doctoral students at Columbia University, the premise of the organization is rigorous, accessible, community-oriented education. Meeting in bookstores, bars, and other public spaces, BISR retains the key element of teaching and learning while shedding the formal structures of educational institutions. This is not to say that BISR's leadership and faculty don't value higher education or the expertise that goes along with it. Quite the opposite: the organization is thriving because so many people outside of universities are hungry to learn. Moreover, the benefits flow both ways. Since 70 percent of tuition directly supports faculty compensation, the instructors are paid a living wage. The accessibility of the courses and the informal setting instill a sense of freedom and openness; many faculty members describe it as the best, most fun teaching experiences they've ever had, with lasting impacts on their research.[5] While there are limits to what can be done in an informal space—nobody can earn a degree through this program, for instance—the model that BISR has created is inspiring in its openness and its focus on engaged, meaningful teaching for public benefit.

The model used by BISR requires a dramatic reframing of the purpose of scholarship, the value of teaching, and the structures that either support or constrain both. In a context such as BISR, public engagement and a sense of career diversity go hand in hand. While faculty in the institute are teaching, their classrooms are in public venues all over the city (and now that BISR has expanded, across the United States). The founders and administrative leadership have had to figure out the details of creating their own organization, from tax law to grant writing to marketing. In doing so, they have in one sense stepped away from universities while remaining committed to very similar goals—and have created new career pathways for many others in the process.

Redefining Research: What Counts?

Opening the academy to new voices and new kinds of knowledge also requires a willingness to see scholarship take on many different formats—far beyond the traditional monograph or peer-reviewed journal article. At the heart of research and publication is the goal of bringing new insight into the body of human knowledge. This central value of making research public is sometimes lost in discussions about scholarly communication, which gets quickly bound up in concerns about tenure and promotion processes and other mechanisms of formal recognition. Refocusing on the creation and dissemination of new knowledge makes it easier to look beyond standard forms and think instead of the ways that research can be most effectively shared with different publics. This happens in different ways—sometimes the best audience to reach is small and specialized, while sometimes it is more powerful to reach a broad, interested public. Digital tools allow us new ways of doing each, and while the form does play an important role in exactly what a scholar can communicate, the particular medium is not typically an end in itself.

One element that is often overlooked in discussing new modes of scholarly communication is the relationship between innovation, equity, and public engagement—all of which can be framed within the understanding of higher education as a public good. Though innovation is often thought of as something for elite and well-funded institutions, through my work with the Futures Initiative and the international scholarly network HASTAC (Humanities, Arts, Science, and Technology Alliance and Collaboratory), I have had the opportunity to think through ways that innovative solutions can be developed organically, out of necessity, to solve real needs and connect communities in meaningful ways. I have seen the ways that teams of faculty, students, and staff across the CUNY campuses have developed cutting-edge digital projects in part to stitch together a diverse and geographically dispersed group of working commuter students. These projects include networked community platforms, collaborative annotation tools, creative pedagogical resources, and more.

The hope of conducting research that has an impact beyond the academy would seem to be something desirable. And yet too often when faculty members work toward the kind of community engagement that can extend the impact of scholarship outside the traditional academic orbit, the work is often not counted in the tenure review process—and is sometimes seen even as a distraction. Several of the scholars whom Patricia Matthew interviewed for *Written/Unwritten* (namely Ariana E. Alexander, E. Frances White, and Jennifer D. Williams) insisted that they did not consider themselves activists, and yet they work persistently and sometimes invisibly to make connections between their scholarly research area and contemporary issues. As Matthew noted, in many ways this ability to connect is not something radical, but simply "sound pedagogy."[6] Bringing the issues of the day into conversation with a literary text from another time or place can help open up the text in new ways, and can enable students to bring new critical insights to the world around them. And yet professors—especially if they are people of color—are sometimes viewed negatively for engaging in such work. The same is true in the potential connections between research and community engagement. Several of the professors that Matthew interviewed indicated that they did not even list such work on their CVs, suspecting it would be considered irrelevant at best.

But deeper connections between research material, communities, and contemporary issues are exactly what a humanities education is about. The scholarly reward structure is currently such that work of this nature is devalued or neutral. How can it instead be incentivized and built into the expectations of what scholarship is and can be? What if, rather than seeing a desire to connect more deeply with the community as a risk or potential distraction from scholarship, such engagement was actively rewarded? This would require a radical reframing of the ways that the university measures and describes success—one that incorporates a far broader and more holistic understanding of the value of research and teaching to society. A more integrative view of the ecosystem in which research and teaching happen—how the community contributes to and is served by the university—may help open the door to research that is deeply grounded in issues that matter to first-generation students and students of color. Such a view would also help to support the public's interest in higher education, which could contribute to stronger state and federal funding. All of these actions would lead to greater diversity among the student body and the faculty, and will increase the number of highly educated people engaged in community leadership.

Meaningful Digital Projects

Sometimes innovation is understood as synonymous with technology. And yet in many instances when discussing changes in scholarly communication or doctoral degree requirements, a focus on technology is—or should be—secondary. The core issue, rather, is one of cultural norms. Technology is in service to the bigger questions of what we want our institutions to look like, and what we are willing to fight for. Change cannot come about if we are too invested in existing systems and structures to step back and try something new. Much of what I advocate in this book requires recalibrating where value is ascribed in the graduate education process, which is undoubtedly controversial and complicated. That kind of careful examination is something that academics excel at in our subject areas, but it is difficult to apply to the medium in which we work. At the same time, working in digital media just for the sake of using technology tends not to yield the most powerful results. Digital work is most compelling when the research question genuinely requires a new way of looking at something. Exploring a new way of presenting research can invigorate a research topic and create a natural avenue for learning meaningful skills.

For instance, consider the work of Amanda Visconti, managing director of the University of Virginia's Scholars' Lab. Visconti's digital dissertation, "Infinite *Ulysses*," is a compelling example of the power of born-digital work.[7] Combining deep literary insight with interface design, web development, community building, and best practices in user testing and analytics, Visconti has created a space for collaborative interpretation of a text. Since its launch, hundreds of readers have annotated James Joyce's text. This and several other examples of deeply creative digital dissertations can be explored through projects such as HASTAC's #remixthediss collection[8] or Alt-Academy's *What Is a Dissertation?* series.[9] The power of networked, peer-to-peer online spaces to share and discuss work is one of the draws of digital publishing. But it is important to keep in mind that online networks grow and thrive the same way they do in person—

they must be built over time. Scholars who cultivate a strong online community are more likely to benefit from the shift toward online public engagement.

This kind of engagement can occur in conjunction with any scholarly work, including those that are relatively traditional in terms of their structure. But what about born-digital publications with complex, dynamic forms that resist the usual structures of articles or monographs? Some platforms, such as Scalar, allow scholars to present research in creative, dynamic, multimodal ways that allow for incredible nuance, insight, and beauty. As one example, artist and educator Evan Bissell and his collaborators created a multimodal project called *The Knotted Line* to examine the history of incarceration, education, and labor.[10] The exceptionally interactive result is something completely different than a traditional article on the same topic would be, even if the research were the same. Another example is the *Torn Apart/Separados* project, a collaborative project that incorporates data visualization, mapping, and narrative to shed light on the 2018 US immigration policy that resulted in the separation of thousands of children from their families.[11] Collaborators used humanities methods and modes of inquiry to scour public data sources and think through questions of ethics, privacy, and historical and political factors, while also drawing on technical skills to build out the site using tools such as Leaflet, d3.js, Jekyll, and Bootstrap. The team also used social media and communications skills to rapidly connect to potential supporters, collaborators, and journalists, which amplified the impact of the project.

Remix the Diss

If equity and innovation are seen as linked, rather than opposed, then it follows that recognizing a broader range of scholarly products makes it possible for scholars with varied backgrounds and skill sets to break new ground—it opens up new avenues so that scholars, departments, or institutions do not maintain the status quo, gatekeeping in ways that allow only certain kinds of people and ideas to advance. As both a capstone of a doctoral student's educational pathway and (often) her first sustained work of scholarship, the dissertation offers a prime opportunity for recalibrating what is considered to be valuable scholarship, interrogating assumed values, and experimenting with new formats.

Scholarly creativity was deeply apparent in a 2014 CUNY event called "What Is a Dissertation," in which graduate students and recent graduates shared projects that looked very different from the typical protomonograph of most dissertations.[12] Some of the dissertations shared during that event, now documented on *#Alt-Academy*, included the use of Tumblr and other social media to share and discuss historical photographs of black women; ethnographic work on contemporary youth created using video and the multimodal platform Scalar; the ecology of proprietary data, explored and shared using mapping visualization tools; a dissertation on comics in comic form; and more. Rigorous, deeply creative work of this nature makes research and scholarship more accessible to broader audiences than ever before—a fact that often brings great joy to the scholar as well.

Rethinking the form of the dissertation and of scholarly communication more broadly can be a question of accessibility, as in the case of Ellen Hibbard. A deaf scholar whose native language is American Sign Language, she wanted the opportunity to share her thinking using the language in which she could express herself most fully—which meant using video. Because ASL is not a written language, she did not want her dissertation to be reduced to a translation into a language not her own. Further, her research focused on the impact of vlogs on the deaf community, and so using video as the medium for her analysis was a particularly useful and meaningful decision. Using video enabled her to write her dissertation in ASL, but also required additional labor above and beyond the typical (and substantial) work of a dissertation. She was required to work closely not only with her advisor and committee to ensure all criteria were satisfied but also with university administration and the library to ensure that her dissertation would be accepted and could be preserved. Indeed, she ended up taking a mixed-media approach, with some video components and some text components, in part because of the need for this translational work. As Hibbard said in an interview, "I had wanted to do it all in ASL, but since this is new and groundbreaking, there were concerns about video not being able to be archived with other dissertation work. The standards for dealing with projects such as mine have not yet been developed."[13]

The structural limitations placed on dissertations at times seem arbitrary, or at least subservient to systems that should not define the avenues available for scholarship; and yet the technical and infrastructural demands Hibbard mentions are not negligible. Some limitations are a factor of what can be accepted—in a purely technical way—into a university's database, typically managed through partnerships between the library and ProQuest, a for-profit service provider. If the existing structures can't accommodate a particular format, graduate students are often discouraged or disallowed from using that format. This remains a challenge even with ProQuest expanding the formats it can ingest, since new accommodations will always be reactive rather than predictive of future needs. Moreover, the preservation of digital work is complicated, requiring regular migration of data to current formats and standards to avoid the risk of having a perfectly preserved and completely inaccessible format. Unlike works that are legible through their physical material, such as manuscripts, digital files are legible only through intermediary technologies that facilitate access. These are constantly changing. The labor associated with data migration and preservation is substantial, and must be a part of the discussion about the forms that scholarship takes and how we can ensure access to future generations of researchers. But databases and repository systems develop around scholars' needs, so scholars should be the ones pushing on the boundaries in order to drive change. This is important for creativity and innovative thinking, and it is equally important in order to allow all scholars' voices and work to be evaluated on their own merit.

In addition to the extra work required to ensure that the medium can be preserved, scholars working in less familiar ways must also make their work legible to the communities that evaluate it, and make the case that unfamiliar structures can in fact offer opportunities for more complex engagement with the subject matter than traditional formats. Scholars are used to reading and assessing articles and books—but the question of how to evaluate a complex, multimodal website is not easy. Sometimes this resistance can be hostile, which is difficult for junior scholars to stand up against. Since more junior scholars (including graduate students as well as untenured faculty members) have the most to lose, they especially need support to do this kind of work—both from individual mentors and from their institutions. For this to happen, formal reward structures must recognize a broader range of scholarship. This means looking carefully at the mechanics of how we accept, process, and archive dissertations; it means examining tenure and promotion requirements and finding new ways to reward innovative work; and it means being attuned to the implicit signals of what constitutes valuable scholarly work and meaningful career outcomes.

The students and recent graduates mentioned above are doing top-notch research and sharing it in ways that make it compelling to a wide audience. And yet despite the excellent examples they shared, there is often continued resistance to recognizing the value of these projects; scholars often must still provide traditional materials as an additional component to their groundbreaking work. Nevertheless, sharing work publicly and collaboratively not only benefits the public but can also serve the individual scholars making their work accessible. For instance, Nick Sousanis, one of the panelists in the "What Is a Dissertation?" event, had a book deal with Harvard University Press in hand before even finishing his dissertation, in part because his (now award-winning) graphic novel *Unflattening* is brilliant and beautiful and innovative, and in part because he had built a strong audience by sharing his work-in-progress online.[14]

The vision for the dissertation is expanding, but much work remains. Collaborative dissertations remain rare, even though deeply creative projects may require many hands. If we want to tackle the most complex questions, we might do well to think of each student's dissertation as one aspect of a larger project, as Todd Presner describes in his notion of the "20-year dissertation."[15] Technologies will inevitably change, so while issues related to building new skills as well as technical affordances and limitations may seem most pressing, questions centering on the purpose and expectations for the dissertation as the capstone of a doctoral degree are more important and more urgent. Exploring these matters also encourages us, as scholars and as readers, to consider what we value in research outcomes.

The dissertation marks the turning point from apprentice to credentialed expert, and so decisions that affect the approach to this project will invariably radiate outward. Looking backward from the dissertation, graduate training may change to better prepare students for opportunities and expectations surrounding the capstone project. Turning to look forward, students' career prospects will change as well, as the differently inflected training and the more public-facing dissertation project will better equip them for a wider range of careers. The skills they gain will help them to become excellent faculty members, too, who can work to further innovate the higher education landscape.

Because graduate school serves a strong socializing and normalizing function, students who try to do something groundbreaking may find that they need to appeal to some kind of precedent to validate their work. While there are incredibly creative projects being done within many graduate programs, it's not always easy for students to find good models. There are risks involved in taking a less customary path, and being able to see what others have done makes it easier for students to assess whether a risk is worth taking. So rethinking graduate training is not only a question of curriculum and professionalization, it is also a question of what models are available to students, and the implicit and explicit messages they hear as they consider their own options.

The desire to share models is one reason that when I first became editor of the online journal *#Alt-Academy*, I developed a new segment that focused on graduate training. The section offers examples of creative research work that students can use as ballast for their own innovative projects. Much like Amanda Visconti's dissertation work, the graduate training section of *#Alt-Academy* focuses both on finished projects and documentation of the process. Guest editors Melissa Dalgleish and Daniel Powell gathered two clusters of material, one that highlights examples of innovative work and another that emphasizes the process.[16] The variety of skills required for the creative projects these students developed, as well as the ability to deftly navigate institutional norms and requirements, are incredibly valuable in career environments. Fostering innovative scholarly work is a key aspect of helping students to be better prepared for a wider range of career possibilities.

The kinds of dissertations that are accepted by an institution send an important signal about what "counts" as scholarly work—a value judgment that extends into the kinds of career paths that are seen as successful outcomes. These value systems have major implications for potential career paths as graduate students engage with new publics in different ways, using different kinds of skills. Changing the evaluation criteria for dissertation projects may not be within the scope of, say, a career center's work, but that center may be able to assess what norms are in place to get a sense of whether graduate students feel they have space to explore new terrain. As new forms of scholarship become more widely accepted, the work that graduate students do will continue to change. When graduate programs offer strong support structures, one result will be students who are well prepared to go into a wider range of careers and have a major impact on the field and on society.

Working Together and in Public

It can be scary to let others see work before it is completely polished, but sharing work in progress can be a valuable way to build readership, solicit feedback, and enable others to see what the research and writing processes can look like. Indeed, many scholars have positive experiences with public engagement both before and after publication. Kathleen Fitzpatrick, media studies scholar and formerly the MLA's director of scholarly communication, has advanced the norms of transparency and collaboration in scholarly publishing by routinely sharing her works-in-progress publicly and inviting feedback. Fitzpatrick has shared entire book drafts online, and because she has long invested time and energy in building an online community, her efforts have yielded a great deal of feedback and conversation. Fitzpatrick has repeated the process with her latest book, *Generous Thinking*, which she shared in draft form for community peer review.[17] This is not only valuable for Fitzpatrick, but it is also a service to other scholars, especially junior scholars, who may feel intimidated and isolated by the daunting prospect of publishing that first book.

This bold approach to sharing middle-stage as well as final work freely has shifted opinions across the profession, giving others a sense of permission to do the same. Fitzpatrick leads by example, exploring topics like technology, publishing, and the academy (as in her book *Planned Obsolescence*),[18] while also building the kinds of social and technological infrastructures than enable meaningful sharing and collaboration. Such projects have included the Institute for the Future of the Book, MediaCommons, and the MLA Commons and Humanities Commons platforms. The Commons platforms create a social network and publication space for members of various humanities professional organizations. They also integrate with a complementary project, Commons Open Repository Exchange, or CORE, that serves as a discipline-based, library-quality repository that anyone in a humanities field can freely use to deposit their own work or read open-access work by others. These innovations require more than just technological expertise and financial resources; they thrive only through a nuanced understanding of the social fabric of academic cultures and norms.

Measuring Success: Prestige or Impact?

For higher education to regain public trust, it must take seriously the mission of serving the public good. As discussed in chapter 2, this includes a critical examination of the formation of a program's student body through the admissions process, its commitment to faculty, the kinds of scholarship it supports, the climate it creates, and the careers that it enables among its alumni. One significant through line that spans these elements is the need to shift the ways that institutions and individuals assign value to scholarly work. Prestige is the coin of the realm in most academic contexts. Is it possible to collectively nudge this standard toward valuing contributions that serve the public good? Since programs naturally compete with one another, shifting the value system to one that emphasizes connection to the community and society can have real effects across the broader landscape of higher education.

Working seriously toward inclusion and support of faculty members who identify with historically marginalized groups, and embracing greater fluidity in the form that scholarship takes, are two key factors for improving the health of the humanities. Because the way we evaluate success is a major factor that prevents progress in these areas, a broader understanding of what constitutes meaningful research or a successful postgraduate pathway may help to slowly change the norms that make it so difficult to advance. By establishing new measures of success—measures that take into account something other than biased student evaluations, or imperfect tenure review processes, or lengthy peer review and publication standards—the humanities open up the possibility of fostering new kinds of scholarship from a wider range of minds.

Opportunities afforded by digital media can be an important part of this effort, since research shared as creative digital work reaches new possible audiences. People who might not have access to scholarly journals, or who might not be inclined to pick up a monograph on a particular topic, might nonetheless spend some time browsing a well-designed interactive website that introduces similar insights. Although complex digital formats do raise questions of longevity and archiving, advantages include the possibility of making work accessible in new ways, as well as creating a different position for the reader—one of active engagement and agency rather than a relatively passive process of consumption. However, work that makes use of innovative formats doesn't always count toward a scholar's professional advancement, and is often done on the margins of more traditional work that is considered safer.

It is already clear that innovative applications of research can be important to the public and valuable to scholars. The next step is to adjust professional reward systems so that projects with significant public impact also garner clear professional merit. Faculty and administrators can also work backward from creative research projects as a way to consider and even reformulate the kinds of training that their graduate programs offer. Most creative projects are not the work of only one person, but incorporate the expertise of many—someone who develops an extensible tool, a developer who customizes it for a new purpose, a designer who determines the best way to present information to a particular audience. With that in mind, programs might encourage more interdisciplinary work as well as increased collaboration. Or research methods courses might be paired with professional development opportunities to learn skills that will allow graduate students to create the best kind of project to suit their research, a strategy I will explore in more depth in the next chapter. Such collaborations and partnerships can enrich the quality, nuance, and impact of a particular project thanks to each collaborator's expertise and perspective, helping the entire project to cohere in a powerful way.

If a program wants to encourage students to take on collaborative, public-oriented work, it also needs to ascribe meaningful credit to that type of research. To begin moving in that direction, there needs to be a conscious decision to start valuing collaborative, interdisciplinary work from students in the early stages of the program. This is equally true in hiring, tenure, and promotion practices. A scholar hired to do innovative work must have the freedom to determine the form that the work will take, and must have the commitment of their program and their university that even when such work challenges the norms established by the program and the university, the scholar must be supported in navigating those processes and in finding ways to ensure that their work is not undermined by rigid limitations. Otherwise, there is a strong disincentive to do anything outside the norm.

The difficulty in changing the metrics of what constitutes successful research and postgraduate pathways has to do with prestige, and is related to the goal of establishing a more diverse and inclusive academic environment. It is complementary to that of broadening career horizons beyond the academy. As long as merit and prestige are measured through the lens of an unquestioned canon and long-standing forms of research and publication, the academy is unlikely to see pronounced *normative* changes in the ways that the humanities are taught and studied, nor in who chooses to pursue such fields of study. If graduate programs genuinely care about inclusion and the new knowledge that it will bring about, graduate education reform must not only focus on broad career options but also—and more importantly—on true antiracist and inclusive practices within the university, as I discussed in the previous chapter.

To be effective, cultural change must come about on several fronts at once. On one hand, the desire for new models must emerge organically from the interests and skills within the academy, especially from graduate students and junior scholars. At the same time, leadership and policies must be in place that support the development of new work and new ways of thinking. And while the most creative work often happens in programs that are not at the center of the national spotlight, it is important that highly prestigious flagship programs also begin to set the tone for change. Graduate programs compete on the level of prestige and reputation, constantly working to attract the best graduate students (a subjective measure, and one that is often regressive in its adherence to traditional definitions of success) and hire the most highly regarded faculty members. If these elite programs (as well as prestigious organizations, such as major funders) can think more broadly about the ways they define success, including whom they recruit and what outcomes they celebrate, other programs will follow suit in an effort to keep up.

If scholarly work that has a clear public value were held in higher esteem within this economy of prestige, graduate programs might also become appealing to a wider range of students who aspire to many different goals. And, if the emphasis on public engagement and applied research was connected with an inclusive approach to recruitment and support, doctoral programs could become a very different kind of community, with a much broader understanding of what constitutes excellence and rigor. Deeper community connections may appeal to students from diverse backgrounds, many of whom find themselves doing activist work simply because of their identities and positions relative to the white, male mainstream of higher education. Making graduate education more inclusive creates the possibility of bringing many new kinds of knowledge into the formally recognized spaces and languages of academia, and takes a step toward establishing greater equity in an environment that has typically favored the elite while purporting to be a public good.

From Individual Success to Institutional Change

Implementing the kinds of changes that are needed in order to shift the cultural norms of humanities programs will undoubtedly be challenging. Many programs face severe budgetary limitations, and simply do not have the funding needed to explore new projects. Faculty members may lack the time or incentives to take on leadership roles or develop new curricula, or may not have expertise in the areas where a department wishes to grow. Similarly, graduate students may know of opportunities that they'd like to pursue, but may lack funding for them, or may be unable to add additional commitments to an already overextended schedule. Both students and faculty members may perceive a risk in exploring opportunities outside the department's standard fare. The structures of hiring, promotion, and tenure often do not reward risk taking of this nature, and students or faculty who do pursue nonstandard opportunities may be called upon to do additional labor to make their work legible to colleagues and evaluators.

Even though these difficulties are very real, a number of programs have taken positive steps toward change and can be looked to as models. As a counterpoint to and illustration of the "Humanities Unbound" study, SCI also established the Praxis Network as a complement to the study.[19] The Praxis Network is a showcase of a small collection of programs that offer creative approaches to methodological training. The initial iteration of the network included eight programs, most of them targeting graduate students.[20] Because the possible approaches to programmatic reform vary widely depending on institutional context, leadership, resources, and more, gathering these programs together and comparing them according to mission, structure, research, the people involved, support, long-term goals, and mechanics allows readers to get a sense of the many ways that creative programming can be embedded in different institutions. Some programs, such as the joint MA/MSc program in Digital Humanities at University College London, are explicitly curricular, having forged new degree programs that build interdisciplinarity into their core structure. Others, such as the University of Virginia's Praxis Program, sit alongside degree programs and offer no course credit, allowing them greater flexibility to explore new approaches and projects.

The Praxis Program, located in the University of Virginia Library's Scholars' Lab, is a useful model to consider. Since 2011, the Praxis Program has selected a small number of doctoral students from various disciplines to work together on a collaborative digital humanities project. Past projects have focused on the challenge of collaborative interpretation of texts, with final products that include tools and games that can be used in classrooms.[21] Students take on roles such as project manager, designer, and developer, and work together to meet deadlines and launch the final project at the end of the year.

The collaborative project may not be directly tied to each student's doctoral research, but the skills that students learn as they work on it have immense benefits to their scholarly work and professional development. Not only are students gaining technical skills through the program, they are also shedding the solitary scholar image in favor of the messy and difficult work of collaborative, interdisciplinary, project-based work toward a real, public deadline. After starting the year by drafting a collaborative charter, students must learn to resolve conflict, navigate varying work styles and preferences, manage competing demands, and share in both challenges and successes. While the program is still recent and many past Praxis Fellows are still working toward their degrees, those who have graduated have gone on to hold interesting, hybrid positions both in and out of universities, as well as more traditional faculty positions,[22] suggesting that the program succeeds in its goal of equipping students for wide-reaching careers in which they will build new systems, both social and technological.

I asked Brandon Walsh, head of student programs at the University of Virginia's Scholars' Lab and former Praxis Program participant, about the significance of the program for his trajectory and his goals as the program's director. For Walsh, the impact of this one-year program was tremendous:

> The Praxis Program completely transformed my thinking about the work that I was doing as a student. I came to the program because I was interested in the kinds of research students in the program were carrying out, but the thing that really stuck was how the work was done. This was new and different than what I had experienced in my academic program. I was suddenly exposed to a commitment to transparent, public work, to an iterative design process, to collaborative project development, and more. . . . In my current role as head of student programs in the Lab, I similarly try to help our students realize that their work, their process, their lives might be different. . . . We try to make our lab a generative space of possibility; to expand options; to say yes, and.[23]

What Walsh describes is a new lens that did not necessarily change the focal point of his studies or career goals, but that enabled him to approach them in a fresh way. The Praxis Program and other programs in the Praxis Network can be thought of as one possible response to the question of how to equip emerging scholars for a range of career outcomes without sacrificing the core values or methodologies of the humanities, and without increasing time-to-degree. The goals of each are student-focused, digitally inflected, interdisciplinary, and frequently oriented around collaborative projects and public engagement. They share similar goals but different structures.

One challenge is how to expand the impact of programs like these to reach a larger number of students. Small extracurricular programs have many advantages; students benefit from strong mentorship and close collaborations with one another when working in small cohorts, and programs that sit outside of traditional departments can allow for greater flexibility and interdisciplinarity. These are great starting points, especially as a means to work within institutional structures (and constraints). However, it also means that programs like these can only reach a limited number of people, making it difficult to achieve true institutional or cultural change. For lasting reform, it will be important to incorporate elements of this type of professional and methodological training into the structure of departments themselves.

Implementing new modes of training within departments will not only help ensure sustainability as programs work to gain a fixed budget line, rather than operating solely or primarily on grant funding; it is also essential in terms of access. Extracurricular programs demand a certain amount of time and flexibility that students with jobs, family commitments, or other obligations may not be able to take advantage of. Building the most innovative work into core departmental programing ensures that all graduate students benefit from the training opportunities. Finally, encouraging graduates to apply their knowledge and methods to all kinds of careers means building important connections with policy organizations, corporations, cultural heritage organizations, and the general public. The deeper those connections become, the more valued graduate education will be, as more people and organizations will be exposed to the kind of high-level and nuanced work that PhD recipients are able to bring to any domain.

When carefully implemented, the practice of greater public engagement and the smart use of digital technology can support broader reform efforts to build greater diversity and true inclusion in the academy. Embedding new knowledge in applied public engagement can be a meaningful way of connecting with communities within and beyond the university, something that may be especially important for students from underrepresented groups. When pervasive bias, ongoing microaggressions, and the serious risk of injustice or even violence at the hands of authority figures are part of a student's lived reality, a course of study that marginalizes those experiences is another instance of systemic injustice and oppression. But if humanities programs can make space to meaningfully explore connections between lived experience and modes of cultural expression, students and faculty members alike might find greater support for their perspectives and contributions—and greater opportunities to thrive.

What Faculty
and Advisors Can Do

The current higher education landscape presents as many challenges as it does opportunities, which can make it daunting to decide where to direct reform efforts. In this chapter and the one that follows, I use the context and arguments of previous chapters to begin building an action plan. First, I turn to faculty members, advisors, and deans of graduate study to offer suggestions both for programmatic change and for better supporting individual students, grounding my advice in the context and arguments of previous chapters. Students will also find this chapter illuminating, as it will provide a glimpse into the concerns and limitations that faculty members face while also suggesting ways forward—topics that students may wish to use to ground discussions with their own advisors. The strategies I offer in this chapter will be complemented by those in chapter 5, which focus more specifically on ways that students can find support, advocate for themselves, and put their PhD to work in a meaningful way.

A growing number of faculty members, as well as graduate programs and professional organizations, are working on interventions that support broader future opportunities for students.[1] These efforts are hugely important—and yet many graduate students still fear that their advisors will not support their consideration of a broad range of professional opportunities. When I visit schools to talk about career pathways, I often find a certain tension among the faculty members and administrators who have invited me or who attend. On the one hand, they are invested in the importance of the topic and, by the simple act of arranging the event or even just participating, they are likely more informed than many of their colleagues on the topic. On the other hand, despite being interested, open, and informed, they often still feel unsure of where to begin. With that tension in mind, this chapter will focus on how faculty members and administrators can take action right now to support both current and future students, through advising and mentorship, curricular reform, connecting with supportive communities within and beyond the university, and tracking alumni outcomes over time.

There are several key principles that undergird the recommendations in this section. One is that graduate programs should not grow beyond what they can ethically and sustainably support. Graduate students work hard as junior colleagues, and their studies and apprenticeship should be compensated as such. If programs cannot provide a funded opportunity for students with adequate mentorship and structure, they should admit fewer students until they reach equilibrium. Doctoral students should not be expected to take out student loans to pay for tuition.

At the same time, expanding access to humanities doctoral study and broadening the view of what constitutes meaningful scholarship would benefit students, the field, and the public. While programs need to provide adequate support, which in some cases means accepting fewer students, reducing the overall number of people with humanities PhDs is not the goal. Trying to reach a balance between the number of graduates and the number of tenure-track jobs by reducing the size of all humanities graduate programs will not solve the jobs issue. The reliance on adjunct labor is not caused by an oversupply of people receiving PhDs, but rather is a separate matter of institutional priorities and cost-cutting that is largely unaffected by the number of doctorates awarded, as I discussed in the first chapter. Moreover, the effects of cutting the size of graduate programs across the board are likely to be detrimental to the overall diversity and vibrancy of humanities programs, as discussed in chapters 2 and 3.

Finally, talking about career pathways is a necessary component of graduate education reform, but it is not sufficient. In particular, any push for reform must include a fight for better labor practices. The current two-tiered system of tenure-track and tenured faculty on one hand, and undersupported adjunct faculty on the other, is detrimental to the learning process and often harms both adjuncts and their students, as I discussed in chapter 1. The structural inequality stems in part from a devaluation of the practice of teaching at research-intensive universities, which is deeply ironic considering that teaching is perhaps the single most central element of education. Because RIs are often seen as more prestigious than many teaching-focused institutions, the values they espouse can be felt throughout the higher education landscape. In particular, the high prestige value of research and publication and the intense pressure that faculty members are under to publish at RIs means that research tends to be showcased while teaching (often) and service (almost always) are pushed into the margins as unpleasant chores. Even the terminology that tends to be used to describe how many courses a faculty member teaches—one's "teaching load" suggests that it is a burden.[2] This is partly tied to gender bias: service work, teaching, and even collaborative research are routinely seen as feminized labor and are subsequently undervalued, as are fields that tend to be more commonly associated with women or femininity (including many humanities disciplines).[3] While teaching-intensive institutions may have different expectations around the balance of research and teaching, there is often still an implicit sense that high-caliber grants and publications carry the most weight. Changing this value system means implementing better recognition and reward structures for teaching and service. As I discussed in chapter 1, meaningful reform does not happen in isolation. The push for broader career preparation will be most powerful if it accompanies support for other efforts, such as improving wages for adjunct faculty, converting adjunct positions to long-term and tenure-line positions, and improving transparency in tenure and promotion processes.[4] These principles of fair labor standards and meaningful recognition of all forms of work inform the suggestions I make in this chapter. I will focus first on the roles of individual faculty members working with individual students, then zoom out to consider opportunities for programmatic change on a broader scale.

Improving Advising and Mentoring

One of the most important things that faculty members can do is help students feel more comfortable talking about career pathways from the moment they begin their program. This costs nothing, and does not require any specialized training to implement. Faculty mentors have an important opportunity to open up these lines of communication with students, and to do so from the earliest days of a student's involvement in the program so that conversations about careers are normalized over a period of several years, rather than rushed at the end. Of course, there are limits to what any single advisor can do or convey, and so mentors can also help students look to a broader community for support and guidance—both within and beyond the university.

As students and faculty alike know well, the support of individual advisors and mentors is crucial to student success. Faculty mentors are deeply trusted voices for graduate students, and the advice that they offer—as well as the unspoken signals—can have a profound effect on students' professional choices. However, in many cases, professional development is treated as something entirely separate from the intellectual work of graduate school (or so deeply integrated as to be synonymous, even though it is clear that many graduate programs do not systematically prepare their students even for academic careers). No matter what is being communicated at an institutional level, or what opportunities are made available, the signals that students receive from their advisors will often carry more weight than what they hear from a centralized, service-oriented space (like a career center, library, or center for teaching and learning—as crucial as these spaces are). After all, it is a student's advisor and department that have the final say in approving their dissertation—and therefore, their degree completion. Central spaces are nonevaluative, which allows them to do many things that academic departments cannot, but also sets them apart from a student's core intellectual work. That separation can create a certain suspicion that thinking about careers is disconnected from—and less important than—talking about research questions. However, when incorporated in a thoughtful and systematic way, thinking more expansively about the ways that graduate programs prepare students for their futures can strengthen students' engagement with the subject matter, methods, and teaching approaches that are core to the academic enterprise. Mentorship from faculty members is a key component of this. Flipping this paradigm in order to understand professionalization as an integral part of how students apply their research and have an impact in the world may mean the topic of career preparation and exploration as a part of mentorship and advisement will resonate more meaningfully with both students and faculty members.

The advising relationship goes well beyond guidance on research and professional development. Advisors can also help smooth the road for graduate students in matters that are not directly related to their studies—for instance, navigating institutional hurdles, understanding tacit rules that govern the academy, and offering insight into confusing or frustrating situations. This is an extra layer of work for advisors—and many times it is largely invisible, emotional labor—but it can be invaluable, especially for students who may be newer at trying to understand the university's structures and politics.[5] For first-generation students and students who identify with underrepresented minority groups, the advisory relationship can either ease or exacerbate points of friction that may hinge on differences of race, class, language, or culture, as I discussed in chapter 2.

Students really need these supportive advising relationships in order to make timely progress toward their degree—not just to support their research, but to support them holistically in the ways that their lives and studies affect one another. Offering such support is in itself a contribution to the student's future career path, as it helps the student to gain confidence, receive feedback in a professional way, and make progress toward a goal. If the student is able to meet interim deadlines and complete a deadline in a timely manner, that becomes a major achievement that the student can point toward in demonstrating their likelihood to succeed on the job. Treating graduate study—and especially the dissertation—in a professional way prepares graduate students to succeed both in their program and after completing their degrees.

Help Students Feel Safe Talking about Careers—from Day One

Students commonly rely on mentoring and advising relationships when they begin considering their career search, but perhaps even more important is the advising that happens in the earlier stages of study. Whether intentionally or not, advising in the first years of graduate school serves to socialize the student into the norms and expectations of the profession. Advising relationships are also one of the key ways in which students learn the "tacit knowledge" of graduate education, as they receive varying degrees of guidance on how to succeed in their discipline: how to write successful conference proposals, fellowship applications, and grants; how to signal their ownership and expertise in an area through word choice, demeanor, and more; and, most simply, how to successfully complete their degree.

Given the depth and breadth of influence that advisors and mentors have on students, it is not an exaggeration to say that for many students, the ability to successfully complete their program hinges on their relationship with their advisor. The high stakes mean that doctoral students worry about pleasing their advisors, and the fear of disapproval about career choices adds to an already sky-high level of anxiety among many—probably most—grad students. The concern is understandable, but it creates a significant problem when it causes a student to avoid the topic altogether, as avoidance only increases anxiety and limits the possibility for solid preparation. When clear communication is lacking, there is much more room for fear, projection, and misinterpretation. The fear of being "found out" or of betraying an advisor is something I hear over and over again from advanced graduate students who are beginning to feel the realities of their impending academic job search more acutely.

Disapproval from advisors can indeed be a real problem. At the same time, some of this anxiety is misplaced, or projected—or simply anticipatory. Most advisors don't want their students to feel ashamed to talk with them about their goals and plans, even if those plans differ from the anticipated faculty route, but without a signal that this is a topic that the advisor is willing to discuss, students may be reluctant to initiate such a conversation. It is important to make it clear to your students that your office is a safe and judgment-free place for them to discuss their goals and future opportunities. Advisors can help their students to succeed by proactively and nonjudgmentally raising the topic of career pathways with their students from the very first advisory conversation, as well as in discussions in group or class settings. Given the high level of anxiety that students experience about the topic of professional pathways, waiting for students to bring up their career interests may mean that the conversation never happens, all while students grow increasingly paralyzed—potentially impacting not only their career paths, but even their degree completion.

The vast majority of advisors really want the best for their students. However, much hinges on what is understood by "best." Two factors often contribute to what students perceive as reluctance or judgment. First, most faculty advisors' own career paths do not include much—or any—experience outside of the university. They typically have deep but narrow experience, having progressed through the familiar pathway of the academy. Even if they wanted to offer their students advice on how to attain their scholarly goals while also opening doors to new and varied opportunities, they rarely have the personal experience that would give them the knowledge and confidence to offer concrete and genuinely helpful suggestions.

Second, and in large part because of the first point, advisors may have a very particular and firmly held idea of what constitutes a successful outcome for their students. When a faculty member is advising a particularly brilliant student, the clearest outcome for success is a tenure-track position, ideally at an RI or a prestigious liberal arts college. In an academic context, this model of success is familiar and well understood, whereas the definition of a "good" nonfaculty position is highly contextual and personal. Watching a student take another path can feel like a loss—the loss of a prospective colleague and of the potential to advance the field. Moreover, faculty advisors may feel they cannot help the student to build a strong network outside of the university; they may not know the players involved; they may not have a clear sense of how their student's strengths map to particular sectors, institutions, or roles. What the faculty member may not be seeing, though, are the ways that the choice of a different path could actually enliven the student's research, benefit the field, and serve a broader public.

Advisors rarely know the full picture of their students' circumstances, and when advisors focus exclusively on faculty careers, they do a disservice to their students. While a faculty position may be appealing in some respects, a student may also be balancing many competing needs and desires: a partner's job, limitations on geographic location, proximity to family, a child's school or caregiving circumstances, health, and many other potential factors.

Even beyond material considerations, a limited message around career pathways may cause students to miss opportunities that they are well suited for and that would be every bit as rewarding as a faculty career. Because the academic job market is centralized and systematized in a way that is rare for most other professions—with job postings available at certain times of the year in certain publications, and with interviews happening all at once at major academic conferences—it can be difficult to undertake other kinds of career searches in parallel. Doctoral students often find the "nonacademic" job market to be unruly, confusing, and difficult to navigate. Hearing an implicit or explicit message that they need not bother is sometimes the only nudge they need to ignore other job opportunities altogether.

This is not to say that every faculty member needs to be an expert in the opportunities available—not at all. Rather, advisors should be prepared for the kinds of questions they are likely to receive, and should encourage students to be self-reflective about their needs and to pursue the resources that are available to help them. This can be incredibly simple—just recognizing that a student may wish to consider other possibilities, and directing that person to relevant resources can go a long way toward enabling a student to feel like a faculty career is one of many possibilities, rather than the only option.

The advising relationship is highly idiosyncratic, and there is really no way to systematize it, given that it depends on the personalities, strengths, and weaknesses of two individuals. Further, no single advisor has expertise in every single area where a student might need support. Even so, developing strategies to influence the discussions around professional development and career pathways that take place in advising relationships may have a profound influence on broader cultural change. I propose offering career advice workshops and training sessions for everyone advising humanities graduate students, in partnership with graduate career offices (where available). Giving advisors the tools they need to make strong recommendations and recognize their students' unique strengths would go a long way toward reducing their reluctance to offer guidance (or simply an open attitude) toward careers beyond the classroom.

If mentors and advisors transmit to students an expansive vision of what scholarly work can encompass, those students are more likely to internalize, enact, and share those same values. With no perceived stigma against career paths in sectors across and beyond the university, students will feel greater freedom to creatively apply their training in a field that makes sense for them. For those who do become professors, they may be more likely to advise their own students in ways that they themselves were advised, creating genealogies of mentorship that embrace a wide range of paths and outcomes.

Connect Students with Supportive Communities

In the best scenarios, an advisor guides a student to greater reflection and self-critique about their research and project development, helps to improve their final product, and offers guidance on professionalization and the daunting steps that follow the dissertation defense. But all of that puts a great deal of pressure on a single faculty advisor, if they are the only trusted voice available. Faculty members (and programs) can also serve their students by cultivating a wider circle of voices offering guidance. There are many people within and beyond the university community to whom an advisor could direct a student for more specific types of support. Graduate career centers are the most obvious example, and are becoming increasingly common across many universities. Situated in different institutional environments—perhaps within central career services, or within the university's graduate school—graduate career centers offer highly trained (and neutral) counselors who work exclusively with graduate students and understand the kinds of roles where they tend to succeed.

Another part of the university community that can offer support for students considering other paths are alumni. If programs value knowing where their graduates' pathways lead, and follow through with a concerted effort to track their students after they graduate, then that alumni network becomes a rich community of people who are likely quite willing to talk with current students from their own program. It also offers students a wider range of models to look to as they consider what the future holds.

A third community that can support the advisor in guiding students are PhD holders who work within the university itself. Every university employs PhDs in a wide range of positions—in the library, in student services, in senior administration, in centers and research initiatives. While care must be taken not to overburden these staff members with uncompensated (and emotionally intensive) labor, they could be a valuable part of the discussion about potential career paths. Whether through direct conversations (in the form of informational interviews, for instance), or via career panels, talks, or other formal programming, the people working within the university can provide a terrific window into intellectually engaging opportunities that graduate students may not have previously considered.

Overall, students need more exposure to people working in different sectors. This could be structured in many ways, from a speaker series to a database of willing mentors to finding ways for students to observe or even work in different settings. Of course, establishing and maintaining the kinds of relationships that would be required for partnerships of this nature takes a great deal of time and care. But, if done thoughtfully, it could be of benefit both to the university and to the partnering organizations. Even directing students to free online resources like Imagine PhD, PhDs at Work, and Twitter hashtags like #withaphd and #altac can offer a low-stakes way of providing students with useful connections, suggestions, and frameworks for thinking about career pathways.

Finally, helping students to establish stronger peer mentorship networks with one another can help create space for informal guidance and advising of a different kind. In addition to encouraging students to form support systems, such as writing groups, within their own cohorts, peer and near-peer mentorship structures can create leadership opportunities for students as they progress to mentor and support incoming students. Not only can more established students help junior students to navigate departmental and university systems, they can also help spark open and nonjudgmental discussions about career opportunities and more. Further, setting up structures that enable students to become leaders within their programs is a tremendous skill that will help them succeed in any career that they choose—both in the classroom and beyond it.

As an illustration of the power of peer mentoring, I would point to the Futures Initiative. Our program's efforts at developing peer mentorship have become some of our most valuable programming, supporting not only graduate students but also faculty members and undergraduate students, many from underresourced backgrounds. One such effort centers on the fact that CUNY graduate students are typically the instructors of record for introductory-level courses across the CUNY system. In the Futures Initiative's first year, we selected three graduate students from a class of ten to run a two-day peer mentoring workshop for CUNY undergraduates, then invited the 350 undergraduate students from all of the graduate students' courses to apply. In the end, we accepted thirty-five students to participate, providing them with transit fare so they could easily reach the Graduate Center, a stipend to compensate for the time they would have to take off from work, and meals during the workshop.

The graduate students carefully planned the structure of the two days in a way that scaffolded the ideas and leadership skills that they hoped students would come away with, while also gradually building in more autonomy so that students could apply those skills as they learned them. During the afternoon of the second day, the graduate students as well as the Futures Initiative staff left the room after charging the undergraduates with setting their own course for how they wanted to connect with their peers in the academic year ahead. When we returned to the room, they didn't notice that we had come in. They were too busy working with each other, discussing ideas and possibilities for what they might do in the future. They built a new website where they could share resources about their colleges and invite questions from their peers. In short, they had fully embraced the idea that they were leaders, that they had skills and knowledge that could be useful to others.

This example focuses on undergraduate students, but the same model applies to anyone. By making it possible for people to lead as well as learn from their peers, we have seen graduate and undergraduate students take charge of their own learning in astounding ways.

Opportunities for Programmatic Change

Tracking Outcomes and Sharing Stories

Whether engaging in small or large reform efforts, programs need data to use as a foundation for their decisions, as well as examples of other programs on which they might model their own. One important way that varied career outcomes can be normalized and celebrated is by simply sharing what those outcomes are. There is a major gap in data about postgraduate humanities pathways, because the humanities portion of the Survey of Doctoral Recipients, the only broad-based longitudinal survey work in this area at the federal level, was discontinued twenty-five years ago, in 1995. Fortunately, in the last few years, a growing number of organizations have realized that there is tremendous value in simply telling the stories of people's career paths. As a result, there is a growing effort to share personal trajectories in an attempt to share models more visibly. Much of this work is taking place within scholarly societies and professional organizations, such as the Council of Graduate Schools, the Graduate Career Consortium, the Modern Language Association, and the American Historical Association. In Canada, a collaborative university-based effort is under way through the Track, Report, Connect, Exchange program (or TRaCE), based at McGill University and a consortium of other Canadian universities. TRaCE pairs an awareness of—and stories about—graduates' pathways with programmatic change. In some cases, the work of sharing pathways and stories has been taken up by private networks and consultancies, such as PhDs at Work, From PhD to Life, and, until recently, Versatile PhD.[6] In addition, recent funding initiatives such as the National Endowment for the Humanities' Next Generation

Humanities PhD program have exemplified the growing need to transform current programs and celebrate—as well as cultivate—broad successes.

Among these efforts, the Council of Graduate Schools in particular has leveraged significant private and public funding to work toward a major, national effort tracking career pathways. Having completed both a feasibility study, funded by the Alfred P. Sloan Foundation and the Andrew W. Mellon Foundation, and a period of survey development, funded by Sloan, Mellon, and the National Science Foundation, the Council of Graduate Schools is now proceeding with a pilot phase (funded by Mellon and the National Science Foundation) in which they will collect information from PhD students and alumni from fifteen institutions.

The fact that such a study is moving forward, and with such varied support from funding agencies, is a hugely important shift. Almost across the board, humanities programs can do a much better job of tracking where their graduates go after they earn their degree; otherwise, any discussion of career possibilities is awash with myth and misinformation. Moreover, the effort to surface not only job titles and institutions but narratives and pathways offers an even more valuable glimpse into how people have gotten to their current positions, and why they made certain decisions along the way.

From a technical perspective, the notion that it is difficult to track people is puzzling. We tend to share more personal and professional data on the internet than ever before, making it easy to conduct a quick search and turn up a LinkedIn profile, an institutional directory, or even a full CV. While 85 percent of graduate deans reported dissatisfaction with the success of tracking former students, and cited lack of current contact information as the greatest hindrance to such tracking, research by a third-party consultancy, the Lilli Research Group, has shown that it is possible to determine the professional outcomes of graduates with a surprising degree of accuracy using only public records.[7] More recently, in a 2018 project called "Where Historians Work," the American Historical Association has documented not only the first job of new history PhDs, but a ten-year trajectory (2004–13) of their professional pathways.[8] Collecting such information is tedious, time consuming, and sometimes resource intensive. But it is not especially difficult. What we lack is collective motivation to value this information, to prioritize its collection, and to devote resources to compiling it in a consistent way. It is important that this effort originates within academic spaces, rather than simply outsourcing it to for-profit platforms like LinkedIn or academia.edu, where that personal data can be sold or shared in unscrupulous ways.

The values of academic programs are on display in the data they gather, share, and celebrate. In a prestige-driven environment like academia, the fact that many programs either do not share career outcomes or only share faculty careers indicates that prestige is located primarily or exclusively in the cycle of doctoral students going into faculty careers. The value other careers might hold—in terms of research impact or individual professional satisfaction—is often far less important in the calculus of enticing a certain kind of prospective student and broadcasting a certain kind of success.

To be sure, some institutions do care a great deal about knowing where their students get jobs. For example, community colleges and for-profit colleges—two very different types of institutions that serve students from similar demographic groups—both tend to be highly aware of alumni career outcomes.[9] Job-seeking and professional advancement is a primary goal for students considering enrollment in for-profits and community colleges, and the schools know it; their success depends on students feeling confident that they can get started in a solid career after graduation. Liberal arts colleges, on the other hand, sometimes give the impression that employment statistics are beneath them and their students—that students should enroll to expand their mind and better themselves, without primary concern for where they will work when they finish. This is often especially true at the graduate level. The privilege of such a stance is enormous. The assumption is that students will do fine no matter what, and that focusing on the material realities of work and wages is somehow unbecoming in the work of the life of the mind. This is the first step to the devaluing of academic and intellectual labor at the postgraduate level.

A glance at many graduate programs' websites reveals a pattern in which certain statistics are proudly shared and others quietly buried. What tends to be emphasized, if anything, are "placements"—faculty positions, especially those at elite institutions. Even short-term lectureships are sometimes shared in these statistics, even though such positions are precarious and can be exploitative. But what about those who become academic publishers, journalists, center directors, policy advisors, museum curators? Unless they were in a program that specifically aimed for those careers as desired outcomes (public history programs are a good example), it is likely that those high-achieving alumni are not listed on the department's website.

One reason for the lack of visibility of people's careers outside the university may be that many departments lose touch with their alumni a year or two after graduation. It is not likely that someone will step into a director-level role immediately upon receiving their PhD; rather, it might take five or ten years before that leadership role is attained. But that is all the more reason to ensure that programs don't lose track of where their alumni are working. What starts as a seemingly uninspiring position may, in time, blossom into an opportunity with incredible impact.

The other reason is that collectively academic programs do not truly and fully see such positions as powerful and meaningful. Moreover, not only are many of these positions important from a public impact standpoint, but in many cases they help to make the apparatus of higher education possible. Academic publishing and librarianship are obvious examples; without publishers, scholars would have no mechanisms to review, polish, publish, and disseminate their scholarship, and without libraries there would be few ways for readers to access that scholarship. But other professions that are adjacent to university structures are similarly crucial to the scholarly enterprise, bringing research and methods into the public sphere and developing new insights that can inform future scholarship.

Narratives of alumni pathways are incredibly important, and not particularly difficult to gather. In fact, one of the easiest (and most cost-effective) things a program can do to normalize a broader range of career paths is figure out who among their alumni is doing exciting work and make those stories visible and celebrated. If programs start doing a better job keeping in touch with their students after they graduate, then that alumni network becomes a rich community of people who are likely quite willing to talk with current students from their own program. Beyond the individual narratives, the collective statistics are important as well. More robust information will make it easier to see and understand the patterns across demographics—race, ethnicity, gender, sexuality, and more—as well as illuminating the arc of people's careers over time. Individual stories are powerful in their own right, but it is the patterns that will better enable educators and administrators to fashion programs that truly foster multivalent success stories in a structural way.

Institutional reward structures are reasonably good shorthand for the values of the academy. Based on what is required for professional advancement and tenure, it is clear that the academy has a hard time knowing how to ascribe professional value to things like service, mentorship, and public scholarship. These elements may not be easy to quantify, and they lack the easy signposting of things like the imprimatur of a highly respected publisher. But that doesn't mean they are impossible to evaluate in a meaningful way. This challenge points to a larger underlying issue: that of prestige and how universities measure success. Prestige is the coin of the realm. Programs continue to emphasize tenure-track placement rates because those are the positions that increase prestige by influencing rankings—and because these kinds of positions are the ones that programs are accustomed to tracking (if any). However, this is not only an inadequate measure of a program's success, but is actually damaging, both to students and to programs. Failing to signal the interesting, challenging work that a graduate is doing beyond the walls of the classroom effectively signals to the former student and their peers that their work is not valued, thereby perpetuating the myth that the only successful outcome is a tenure-track job. Further, it's a missed opportunity for programs, since the public—including prospective students—greatly values and esteems a wider range of work. If a program's graduate is working for a nationally celebrated public radio program, that is as good an indicator of their success as a faculty position would be—and garners admiration from those for whom academic markers of success are not the only ones that matter.

Incorporating Professional Development

One of the biggest issues with career preparation in graduate programs is that it often starts far too late, when students are at the dissertation stage and thinking actively about what their next steps will be. By that point, students who are interested in other opportunities and skills may feel like the rug has been pulled out from under them, and indeed there may not be time for someone to gain the kinds of experience they might need in order to be competitive for a range of roles. With that in mind, my strongest suggestion to faculty members is to begin planting the seeds for career preparation and professionalization as early as possible.

There are competing demands that make the goal of early preparation difficult to achieve. With many interventions in graduate program structures focusing on reducing time-to-degree, adding something new can be a tough sell. Rather than adding, though, a certain amount of what I propose could be accomplished through new approaches within existing systems. Seen this way, career preparation is a deepening of the kinds of skills and approaches that programs already offer, rather than a departure. The results of the SCI "Humanities Unbound" study showed that once people are in new careers, they often realize that they are continuing to use the skills and knowledge from their doctoral studies in unexpected ways. Notably, regardless of respondents' primary responsibilities, many reported that they still engaged in some type of research or teaching. Just over half of respondents (51 percent) continue to teach in some way, while an even greater proportion, 68 percent, perform research as a part of their job. Many (61 percent) also pursue these activities outside their position.[10]

Incorporating professional development into the core intellectual work of doctoral education is not only possible, but can foster excellent research and timely degree completion. I discussed the importance of rethinking the structures and platforms of scholarly work in chapter 3; reform of this nature is also an important component of how faculty can better support students in their academic and professional pursuits. Take the dissertation as an example. The humanities dissertation often assumes a particular form—the protomonograph—and writing it can be a deeply isolating or even a disheartening experience. Yet the issues raised, the implicit audiences, the stakes of the arguments—none of these are intrinsically bound to a particular form, and indeed scholarship may be greatly enriched by moving beyond the conservative containers that constrict our most advanced and groundbreaking thoughts. Enabling and encouraging graduate students to craft a dissertation project that is suited to their research topic as well as to their own skills and work styles can lead to surprising and exhilarating new work. Even minimal flexibility, such as allowing the dissertation to take the form of a collection of articles rather than a single cohesive book-like structure (already widely accepted in a number of STEM and social science fields, but relatively uncommon in the humanities), can help students to make steady progress while still engaging in rigorous research and analysis. Such flexibility also puts more ownership in the hands of the student, and carries with it the expectation of clear project management—determining an appropriate scope for the project, setting a timeline, and sometimes collaborating with others. With no sacrifice to the intellectual work, students gain valuable skills for any workplace and may even feel a greater sense of joy in their work. A critical consideration of core elements of humanities graduate training—things like research methods, archival practices, close reading and analysis, cultural understanding, writing, and more, depending on the field—can help move beyond the particularities of structure and tradition and distill core values that can be applied more flexibly.

Changes like these not only help students to develop new skills but also, perhaps more importantly, make it easier for them to see connections between those skills and different ways they might be applied. Even on an assignment level, projects that encourage more critical inquiry into matters of audience, project management, and collaboration can be invaluable. To expand the knowledge and skills gained through writing a research paper, faculty could consider adding a public component to course projects that requires students to reframe their argument toward a different type of audience. For instance, students might build a website that considers the implication of design in the way readers approach a text. Or they could pitch versions of their scholarly work to nonspecialist publications—perhaps developing an op-ed for a local paper, or a deep dive into a humanities topic with current relevance for an online magazine. Students in social sciences might develop policy briefs or community resources that build on their research and analysis. Such projects insist on deep mastery of content and research methods, while also helping grad students learn to take on varied roles, acquire new skills, and key their work to different kinds of audiences.

At the same time, graduate students often need practice in translating or reframing their skills in language that resonates with prospective employers in different industries. One aspect of career training that would be beneficial to graduates is learning how to recast their skills. For instance, a dissertation may be more interesting to a potential employer if it is framed as a complex, long-term project involving research, written and oral communication, and a series of deadlines completed on time. Further, the core skills of graduate training—especially research, writing, and analytical skills—are highly valuable to employers, and often enable employees to learn new skills quickly.

Because the processes and products of skills like teaching and research can seem foreign in new employment environments, it is critical that students don't undervalue (or insufficiently articulate) the ways that graduate study equips them for other roles, particularly in terms of methods and generalized skills that can be broadly applied. Respondents in the "Humanities Unbound" study noted that in their roles, teaching and research often differ significantly from the usual forms they take in academic settings, and are frequently much less formal. Activities that feel much like teaching may be described as presentations, mentorship, and management. Research may be fast paced, requiring that one seek out and synthesize information quickly in order to facilitate decision-making. Other skills, like navigating complex university bureaucracies, creatively solving problems, and adapting to unexpected circumstances, are not explicitly valued within the educational system but are nonetheless powerful and broadly transferable skills that can be the difference between surviving and thriving in other employment contexts.

Rethinking Core Curricula and Methods Courses

In addition to rethinking the kinds of scholarly project opportunities available to students during their studies, another way to build in better preparation for a wider range of careers from the very beginning of a degree program is to take better advantage of methods courses. Incoming students are highly sensitive to learning their department's expectations, so the first semesters are a key moment to demonstrating that a program takes an expansive view of why graduate study matters and how it can be applied. And yet methods courses are often ad hoc and idiosyncratic, even within a single department, depending on the faculty member who happens to teach it in a particular semester—and nearly 30 percent of humanities doctoral students report that their departments offer no methods courses at all.[11] While these courses do often teach valuable disciplinary foundations and research methods, more than anything they often serve as a socialization course, showing students the norms and unspoken expectations of the discipline. Given that, it is a prime opportunity to rethink the norms that new graduate students are learning, and to start providing not only skills but also implicit support for public engagement and broader application of educational training.

A more thoughtfully designed "keystone" course (to complement the dissertation capstone) would not need to sacrifice the essential content—research methods and disciplinary foundations. Rather, it could teach that content using approaches that implicitly show the value of collaborative, project-based, public-facing work. In a blog post that proposes killing off methods courses in the way that a gardener might uproot weeds to make room for fragile seedlings to grow, Bethany Nowviskie reimagines methods courses that not only prepare students for the academic trajectory that lies ahead but also enables them to "feel *empowered to build and re-build* the systems in which they and future students will operate."[12] A common first-year course across a cluster of departments that introduced students to the structures, power dynamics, and key challenges of higher education alongside research skills would be eye-opening for most students, and would put them on a better footing for their degree and for a wide range of leadership opportunities thereafter.

By rethinking core curricula in such a way that graduate students gain experience in skills like collaborative project development and public engagement, departments would be strengthening their students' future prospects regardless of the paths they choose to take. While students are generally well prepared for research and sometimes for teaching, they aren't necessarily ready for the service aspect of a professorship, which incorporates many of the same skills that other employers seek. Collaboration and an understanding of group dynamics, for instance, would help committee members to work more effectively together. Many of the skills also contribute to more creative teaching and research. Better project management would help faculty to make good use of sabbatical years and to balance the anticipated fluctuations in workload, while technical knowledge would lead to new kinds of assignments in the classroom and new research insights. And yet these skills are not typically taught as part of the graduate curriculum. Methods courses, which could be used as an opportunity to introduce students not only to the critical skills and approaches they will need but also to key issues of professionalization and postgraduate realities, are inconsistent and sometimes completely absent.

It is not surprising that employers find that humanities-trained employees need to develop or refine skills like project management and collaboration. Employees themselves also recognize that these are by and large not skills that they acquire in graduate school—at least not through the official curriculum of their graduate programs. Skills like collaboration, project management, interpersonal skills, and technical skills are all valuable in a range of career paths that attract humanities scholars, but graduate programs do not typically prepare their students in these areas. Even those who felt that their skills in these areas were strong noted that they gained them outside of their graduate program— for instance, through jobs or internships. Graduate programs could include opportunities to learn and apply these kinds of skills by partnering with organizations willing to host interns, or by simulating a work environment through collaborative projects with public outcomes.

Career-related reform efforts in doctoral programs are not a new idea. On the contrary, some institutions, funding agencies, and individual researchers have been working on such reform for decades. Maresi Nerad, professor emerita at the University of Washington, has conducted vital research on doctoral education and career pathways since the late 1990s, including a survey of PhD holders ten years after degree completion.[13] Around the same time (from 2000 to 2005), the Woodrow Wilson Foundation established the Responsive PhD program, a comprehensive, multi-institutional effort that engaged graduate deans at twenty institutions across the country in significant programmatic interventions to support adventurous scholarship, new pedagogical practices, greater diversity and inclusion in the academy, and community partnerships.[14] More recently, the Humanities Without Walls program (supported by the Andrew W. Mellon Foundation beginning with a planning grant in 2012), a consortium of fifteen midwestern institutions, offers predoctoral workshops in career diversity and collaborative research opportunities centered around grand challenges research. The impressive work of participating programs, such as the University of Iowa's Obermann Center and the Humanities PhD Project at the University of Michigan, are amplified and strengthened through the collaboration. The programs highlighted by the Praxis Network, which I discussed in chapter 3, are also excellent examples of fresh, high-impact thinking in graduate programs.

This constellation of reform efforts is impressive and gives much hope. How can we collectively move from grant-funded efforts to lasting cultural change? Relying on external funders presents challenges to sustainability, since grants come to an end and funding priorities can shift. For example, in 2016 the National Endowment for the Humanities launched a $1.7 million matching grant program, called the Next Generation Humanities PhD, that envisioned similar reform efforts. The program, however, was short-lived, ending after two cycles of planning grants and a single cycle of implementation grants. This highlights a key challenge facing many innovative doctoral programs: often, the most groundbreaking work is funded by grants, making sustainability and longevity a real challenge. Fortunately, the work of graduate education reform continues through a number of other avenues, including other funding initiatives, major institutional efforts, and smaller, grassroots programs (sometimes spearheaded by a single faculty member looking to better support their students).[15] A key goal moving forward should be to find ways to support such efforts through stable institutional budget lines in order to have a lasting impact.

Community Partnerships

In addition to curricular reform, another powerful avenue for change involves looking outward—to organizations and companies that benefit from partnerships with graduate programs. While research and teaching assistantships are long-standing and valuable channels for a certain type of professional development, there is room for much more creativity in the ways that student positions that offer tuition remission and funding are structured. For some students, a part-time position in an organization outside the university could provide valuable job skills, an important network, and a sense of how the skills and knowledge they are gaining through their studies might be applied in a very different setting.

For such apprenticeship-style positions to be mutually beneficial, strong and clear partnerships are needed between university programs and companies or nonprofit organizations in the surrounding community. Taking on new staff with limited experience can be a drain on the organization, but if care is taken to work with leadership at those organizations, it is possible to build in reciprocal arrangements that are valuable to them. In some cases, it might be that employees at the partner organization would like to be able to take courses within the department. In other cases, the organization might wish to have someone from their staff teach a course from time to time, thereby baking in the development of skills and perspectives that the organization finds important.

In return, it is important that the organization have a clear role in mind for any students who may be embedded there. Perhaps students can take ownership of a particular project, or conduct a series of "rotations" that allow them to see the full picture of how the organization works. Ideally, the position should also be incorporated into the student's research in some way—perhaps the role will come to influence their dissertation topic, or they may shift their research goals based on what they learn. Those kinds of connections should be encouraged. One way to do so would be to have students write frequently and publicly about their experience.

In many universities in Canada, as well as some in the United States, the co-op model of education does exactly this, though more commonly with undergraduate education rather than doctoral programs. Co-op programs, for instance at the University of Victoria, British Columbia,[16] or at Northeastern University in Boston,[17] provide paid employment, course credit, skill development, a network, and a chance to explore different career opportunities. Thanks to funding from the Mellon Foundation, the Graduate Center has implemented a program of this nature through PublicsLab, a new center designed to expand career horizons while also supporting publicly engaged research. In a program that is well established, such as the one at the University of Victoria, the university also offers the support typical of a career services office—helping students to discern their strengths, matching them with possible opportunities, and offering workshops and guidance to help them succeed.

Many work opportunities in programs like these are local (some even within the university), but others are built on national and international partnerships, allowing students to apply for positions relevant to their studies that may be place-specific. For example, Rowan Meredith, a Slavic studies student, spent a term working in the Auschwitz-Birkenau State Museum in Poland—something that had direct connection to her expertise and research interests.[18] At the graduate level, some of the University of Victoria's co-op placements have included work at the United Nations headquarters in New York; program administration for Nepal- and Australia-based nonprofits working on Nepali migrant workers' rights; and a placement with an indigenous law co-op in Canada.[19] To gain these opportunities as a fundamental (and funded) part of one's studies, rather than have to break with one's program in order to pursue them, is a huge advantage for students who wish to pursue any pathway—even a faculty career—as it gives them a chance to see and experience other employment environments and test out whether they might fit.

Modifying the ways that graduate students can receive funding will help them to explore opportunities, build a network, and gain skills and experience that will make their résumés more competitive for positions when they complete their degree. In the current system, by contrast, students may complete their degree without having much or any job experience, meaning that they may need to start in an entry-level job, where their deep educational background may make them seem paradoxically overeducated but underprepared. Some programs actively discourage or forbid their students from taking outside employment, and international students are often unable to work while pursuing their studies, which makes it extremely difficult to gain professional experience prior to graduation. The sense that one may need to take an entry-level job also fuels the feeling that taking a job outside of the classroom is not a successful step. Many do find that they are able to advance quickly once they take the first step, but it makes far more sense to gain experience early, when the stakes are not as high.

Suggestions for Getting Started

There is much work to be done at the level of both individual faculty members and of departments or programs. The following suggestions offer starting points for those whose programs may just be beginning to have conversations about expanding the notion of successful postgraduate career pathways, as well as more complex and resource-intensive ways to continue that work once a program has shown a willingness to move toward lasting structural change.

For individual faculty members:

→ Build trust with your students and use that trust to help them explore meaningful opportunities.

This is perhaps the single most important step, and one that can be taken immediately, regardless of institutional context or available resources. In advising students, take care not to implicitly convey that a faculty career is the most important sign of success. Take care not to inadvertently shame students who consider more varied pathways; on the contrary, do all you can to normalize and valorize such considerations. This can happen through individual advising conversations, classroom discussions, and through the kinds of programming a department offers. If you feel unable to offer advice on a particular matter, point students toward resources or people who may be better positioned to help.

→ Encourage (and if possible, provide funding for) students to become members in relevant professional associations, even if the students do not intend to pursue careers as faculty.

Professional associations can provide useful opportunities for networking and professionalization that extend beyond the limitations of an individual department. Some, such as the American Alliance of Museums or the American Association for State and Local History, offer professional development opportunities more specifically geared toward careers in various realms of public humanities.

For those with input into programmatic decision making:

→ Consider evaluating and modifying required aspects of master's- and doctoral-level curricula in favor of including courses that help students to prepare for the wide-ranging career paths that they may pursue upon completion.

This is not to say that graduate programs should become vocational training grounds; rather, this recommendation encourages programs to reconsider the ways in which they currently train graduate students for a single career path—that of the professoriate—and instead broaden the scope of training in order to reflect more accurately the postgraduate realities of their students. Incorporating such training will better equip students for any career—including the professoriate—without detracting from more traditional methodological training. In fact, done well, helping students to learn some of the critical skills that are widely legible and valued in professional environments (like collaboration and project management) can actually deepen their grasp of standard disciplinary methods.

→ Rethink standard methods courses to structure them around a collaborative project in which students must apply a range of skills toward an end goal centered on methodological understanding.

Such a project would not only guide students toward the disciplinary framework that they will need throughout their degree program, but would also enable them to learn and apply skills that will improve their research skills and future employment prospects. Good data management habits, project planning, collaboration skills, and more will have immediate value as well as future value. Such courses could even be transdisciplinary to encourage critical thinking about field-based assumptions and theoretical lenses.

→ Create one-credit courses that center on ecosystems crucial to the academic landscape, such as scholarly publishing.

Graduate students wishing to pursue an active research career will benefit with a greater understanding of traditional and emerging publishing options, and best practices for planning, research, writing, and submitting scholarly articles. Students uncertain about what career they wish to pursue, or those explicitly interested in alternative academic career options, will also benefit from a greater understanding of the research and publication environment, a sense of existing platforms and opportunities for new developments, and a deeper understanding of broader academic structures, which many employers and employees have noted is valuable.

→ Form more deliberate partnerships with the inter- and para-departmental structures—either within or outside your home institution—that are already engaging in this kind of work.

Humanities centers have jump-started excellent training programs, research projects, and public-facing work. For example, under the direction of Kathleen Woodward, the Simpson Center for the Humanities at the University of Washington offers a cross-disciplinary Certificate in Public Scholarship, numerous fellowships, and a slate of public programing; the center has also cultivated numerous campus-community partnerships.[20] The reports from SCI's meetings on graduate education reform highlight a number of similarly strong examples, as well as future possibilities.[21] Departments that would like to move in similar directions can model the kinds of programs being offered by these centers, and might also consider pursuing interinstitutional collaborations as appropriate. There may be valuable opportunities to share infrastructure (physical and digital), expertise, time, and funding across multiple institutions, as a new partnership between Hope College and Michigan State University demonstrates.[22] Departments, libraries, and centers should model the best practices they hope to teach to their students: collaboration, equal credit, public engagement, and transparency.

→ Cultivate partnerships with the public sphere, both to provide graduate students with valuable experience and exposure and to make a clearer case for the public value of humanities education.

Many respondents cited an internship or previous employment as crucial to their current position, yet graduate programs more often encourage students to remain cloistered within the confines of the department. Departments could build alliances with local cultural heritage organizations in their city or town—such as museums, libraries, and archives—and work with students to engage with those partners either through their research or through short-term employment or internships.

→ Critically examine the kinds of careers that your program implicitly and explicitly promotes, and consider ways to increase the visibility of the varied paths that scholars pursue.

One way to do this is to compile lists of people working within the university system that hold advanced degrees, so that students can see potential paths and make useful connections. Stanford has taken positive steps in this direction by listing staff members who are willing to serve as mentors to humanities doctoral students, and by developing a speaker series to highlight the varied careers of these members of their community.[23]

→ Make a much stronger effort to track former students (including those who may not have completed a degree), and to encourage current and prospective students to connect with former students.

At present, very little data is available from departments about the career outcomes of their graduates.[24] While social media can provide a surprising amount of information about former students' current careers,[25] concerted efforts from departments and professional organizations are critical to standardizing the process to make it easier for prospective students to compare results across institutions. Doing this work retroactively is a major undertaking; making it a routine part of departmental expectations would make it much less labor-intensive. Robust, standardized tracking would also make it possible to compare the results of different kinds of programs in order to better evaluate the effectiveness of new models.

Faculty members, advisors, and administrators have a vitally important role in changing the ways that students and institutions perceive career diversity, even if their own professional experience has been exclusively within a university setting. The opportunities for intervention range from modest individual efforts to major systemic changes. Reform might start small, perhaps by changing the ways careers are discussed in mentoring relationships, or offering project-based or public-oriented assignments in graduate courses. At a structural level, working toward broader curricular change and fostering partnerships with organizations outside the university can open the doors for public engagement and deeply creative scholarly work, while also creating organic opportunities for students' individual growth. When students feel well supported, they do their best work—whether that work takes the form of traditional scholarship, or something that breaks the mold in new and exciting ways.

Students: How to Put Your PhD to Work

If you're a student or recent graduate interested in exploring broader career paths and have picked up this book as a result, know that you have already taken an essential first step. The act of exploration and self-awareness in itself is a valuable step to help you prepare for your future—no matter what career you ultimately pursue—and the preceding chapters offer a solid grounding in the current academic landscape, the stakes of structural reform efforts, and ways that faculty members and administrators can make a difference. To complement that foundation with practical strategies, in this chapter I will offer suggestions for taking control of your own pathway. This chapter is not only for students, though; if you are a faculty member looking for new ways to advise students with varied goals, this chapter will give you concrete tools to better support your students.

At a moment when people and places around the world are becoming more deeply interconnected, and technology is becoming a more intimate part of many lives, bringing a humanities background to contexts beyond the university can foster greater critical engagement and cultural understanding in high-stakes environments. With that context in mind, this chapter will focus on practical suggestions, ways to begin preparing for future careers at any stage of a doctoral program, and how to succeed academically while also creating and taking advantage of opportunities that go beyond the classroom. I'll address questions related to the job search and interview process, from assessing personal needs and desires to navigating a set of workplace cultures that can be quite different from that of the university. Because the dissertation is often the most concrete marker of a PhD, and one that offers a way to explore not only new ideas but also new kinds of research and writing, I will also focus part of this chapter on matters related to the dissertation—including public engagement, digital and other nonstandard formats, and measures of success.

One of the most common questions I hear from doctoral students when I talk about this topic—whether at a vast public university system like CUNY or an elite private Ivy League institution like Yale—is "how do I know how much preparation is enough?" It's no surprise that this would be a pressing concern; doctoral students are under a tremendous amount of pressure, face a high degree of uncertainty about the future, and in many cases feel that the system has failed them despite every effort and achievement. They want to make themselves competitive for as many avenues as possible, and yet also worry that their faculty mentors may not approve of career pathways outside the classroom. Many students hear conflicting messages, with some faculty members encouraging them to focus and others (or the noisy world of social media) urging them to pursue new skills and cover their bases. Students are pouring their time, energy, and resources into their work while wondering what awaits them when they finish. It can be paralyzing—which is why breaking the topic into manageable steps is so essential.

One thing to keep in mind—something I find reassuring, though it might first seem daunting—is that in any new position, there will be many, many things that you don't know. As early modern literature scholar Sarah Werner told me,

> The most challenging thing about starting my first job was recognizing that I wasn't expected to be an expert in one narrow area but to learn on the job a wide range of academic areas. I'd been trained to do one tiny thing very, very well; now I know lots of fields, but none of them as in-depth. In other words, I spent a lot of time at first feeling nervous about how much I didn't know; now I realize it's okay not to know things, since the skill is learning them, not already knowing them.[1]

While it can seem scary not to be an immediate expert, especially for people with a high level of expertise and competence, it is wonderful to know that all employers expect you to have a ramp-up period, during which you are learning and acclimating. It also means that opportunities to grow and learn will be a part of your future, even after your days as a student are done.

Knowing where to begin can be one of the most vexing questions for humanities graduate students. Talking about careers sometimes feels like a departure or even a betrayal, something that must be done furtively to avoid arousing suspicion. And yet there are so many career paths that not only align with but *amplify* the goals of doctoral study in the humanities. Keeping this in mind and starting with a mentality of affinity rather than opposition may help resolve some of the tension bound up in considering possibilities for the future. One way to do this is by focusing on core values—such as research, teaching, and impact—that are central to scholarly work and can be easily understood across different professional contexts.[2] In an academic context, research is typically assigned the highest value, bringing new insights and new lines of inquiry into the field. Teaching may be highly valued as well, especially at places like small liberal arts colleges and community colleges; such teaching-focused institutions know that thoughtful teaching sparks students' curiosity and prompts them to make connections in their own lives. Underlying both of these values is a third, less commonly articulated value that gives purpose to the work and yet is hardest to define: impact, or connection to the broader world beyond the narrow radius of a single department, university, or discipline. Formal designations of scholarly impact can include relatively quantifiable markers—like citations and grants—but also more elusive signs of influence within and beyond the academy that are almost impossible to measure. Impact might take different forms, such as signs of engaged readership (through social media activity, comments on an article, and so on), a thriving or profitable organization, a change in local policy, a widely used website or resource, and much more. Citations are only one small way of showing that your research matters.

Working within the existing value structures of academic programs means that making your work legible is more a matter of translation than complete reconfiguration. Focusing on these three values—research, teaching, and impact—provides a starting point for the translational exercise of reframing the skills and outcomes of a humanities PhD into terms that resonate with a wider range of potential employers, starting with skills *you already have*. For instance, research requires project management skills and the ability to assemble and articulate a robust argument. Teaching requires careful planning, communication, public speaking, and assessment, as well as an ongoing act of listening to and translating for nonspecialist audiences. And while impact is often considered *within* a single field, that is arguably too narrow a scope; the most powerful scholarship leads to new policies, institutional structures, technologies, public engagement, and more. Being able to see the potential for how scholarly work can be framed within these three overarching values will make that work more powerful in any context. No matter what kind of career a student hopes to pursue, conducting this translational work can help surface unrecognized skills and achievements.

For most graduate students, there is likely a connection among these three values that acts as a kind of driving force, though it can take some deliberate time for reflection to articulate exactly what that is. Students, try to set aside time to work on this, asking yourself questions about what you find most meaningful in your work, why it matters, what keeps you going when you feel stuck or discouraged, and whose voices you hear when you imagine feedback from the audiences you consider most valuable. (Advisors, you can help your students by asking them these questions as well, and by listening to what they say.) Since the answers will undoubtedly change over time, consider returning to these questions throughout your career as a way of checking in on the underlying values of your work. Research and teaching that connect directly to matters of public concern, for instance, imbue humanistic scholarship with greater urgency and relevance. As an example, the recent push to teach materials that offer cultural and historical context and perspectives on movements such as Black Lives Matter enables students and researchers both to make more meaningful connections between contemporary antiracist activism and the study of art, literature, history, and other forms of cultural expression. That connection and urgency may be highly motivating; or, there may be other factors that drive your research. Working within both the explicit and tacit value systems of the academy, and of the humanities more specifically, consider how you can make the most of your PhD program in a way that prepares you not only for the rigors of a faculty career but also for a much broader array of possibilities.

The Art of Translation

As subjective—and perhaps maddening—as it sounds, the frame of mind with which you approach your job search can have a huge effect not only on your well-being, but on your likelihood of success. Potential employers can easily spot someone who is applying for a position while considering it an unpalatable backup plan, and will be unlikely to want to bring that person into their workplace as a colleague, no matter how much experience and education they have. On the flip side, genuine enthusiasm can shine through in a well-written letter or during an in-person meeting, and can make it more likely that the prospective employer will want to take a chance on a candidate, even if their experience doesn't align precisely with the standard pathway into a particular job or field.

Even when you are deeply enthusiastic about an opportunity, knowing how to get started and how to make yourself competitive can be challenging, especially since there are often very few models that you can look to among your peers or trusted advisors. The most important and challenging element can be considered a work of translation—showing a prospective employer exactly how your experience within academia can be an asset within a very different context.

I have suggested that focusing on research, teaching, and connection—or impact—may be a useful way to frame both the skills you are gaining in your doctoral program and the kinds of work you may wish to do when you finish. Here's a bit more of what I mean by that.

How Research Matters in the Workplace

The bread and butter of doctoral work is discovering, reading, and analyzing large volumes of complex information. PhD students are constantly learning new material, interpreting it, determining what is important, and synthesizing new findings in clear and thoughtful writing. Because graduate school is in an environment where this work is common and expected, it can be hard to see that this is something that can be distinctive in many professional contexts. Research and writing skills are unbelievably valuable in almost any career.

In addition, if you have applied for funding—whether competitive national fellowship opportunities, modest internal travel grants, or something in between—you also have experience taking your research to a new level by translating its importance to an unfamiliar audience. Blogging exercises the same muscle, albeit with different stakes. This skill of conveying the potential impact of research is crucial once you step beyond your home department. It takes a great deal of confidence (and a good ear for tone) to shift the register of your work from the specialized language of your subfield to that of a more general audience. The ability to do it well is something that can set you apart in your application materials, as well as in different career environments.

In my research, I have found that many PhD holders working outside the classroom tend to undervalue their research skills, whereas their employers find it to be one of the PhD-holders' strongest attributes. I suspect this may be because the process and product of research outside a familiar university setting may look quite different, leading PhDs to overlook the fact that their studies provided them incredible preparation to do sophisticated analysis on unfamiliar materials.

Moreover, your research skills are by no means limited to a particular subject area. You can—and should—apply research skills to the job search itself. Not only can you flaunt your research skills in a cover letter or interview, you can also use them to find the opportunities that might be worth applying to in the first place. Approach your search as you would a research question—with curiosity, close reading skills, an eye for patterns, and perseverance. Start with broad keywords just to see what emerges; this might be a title ("coordinator," "research associate," "program director"), a skill or content, or an organization. Then, ask yourself what sounds interesting, challenging, tedious, or intriguing about what you find. Even if a job description seems like a stretch in terms of the type of work or the depth of experience required, ask yourself how the skills or tasks sought in the ad might connect to your own background, and to a bigger picture that you find meaningful. The results can be surprising.

Teaching beyond the Classroom

As a graduate student, you have been steeped in an environment of formal teaching and learning for years—even decades, going back to the earliest grade-school years—and have therefore seen many, many teachers at work. If you have taught courses during grad school, you have had the opportunity to see teaching and learning from both perspectives, as both learner and as teacher. You have perhaps crafted a syllabus, created assignments, evaluated student work, and helped coax reticent students to trust their voices. Classrooms are a space you know deeply.

But teaching can happen in countless ways, both formal and informal; it is not limited to the classroom. In fact, it is very likely that you will engage in some form of teaching no matter what career you choose. Creating workshops or training plans, presenting material to colleagues, guiding and mentoring a junior staff member, bringing senior leadership up to speed on an issue you know well—all of this requires the same kinds of skills that you know from your experience in the classroom.

Translation is important here as well. One of the key things that teachers do well is translate complex material in such a way that students can learn, little by little, as they build confidence and gain insights. Outside of classroom settings, this is more likely to happen in one-on-one or small group contexts—which can often be even more rewarding than teaching to a full class.

Teaching also draws on project management (and people management) skills, as you build a semester-long course in which individual lessons and assignments lead to certain learning outcomes, and as you guide students toward reaching these goals. Starting with a big-picture goal and an end date and working backward to determine a reasonable pace is something that you will do in many careers. Too often, though, we forget that teaching includes these kinds of skills. Even though the language used in different professional contexts may be unfamiliar, the mind-set and approach used in teaching is something that you can undoubtedly draw on. Need to present material to the board? Help a colleague learn a new skill? Convince leadership of the merits of a particular approach? Teaching skills will propel you.

Articulating Impact and Connection

The potential impact of scholarly work is the trickiest piece to define, but arguably the most important to keep in your sights. Impact has a great deal to do with connection. As an emerging scholar, you learn how to draw connections among people, movements, ideas, and more. You enable your students to seek and articulate these connections, and to see and create meaning based on their lived experience. And yet sometimes that ability to connect is forgotten, even in the act of scholarly writing. If the skill is sometimes overlooked in core academic work, it is even more likely to be invisible as you seek careers where the applications of your skills may be less readily apparent. And yet that possibility for connection, for meaning, and for the creation of new knowledge can be even more powerful when you are engaging with publics beyond the formal classroom. Your scholarship and expertise can have a profound impact when brought into conversation with the varied perspectives, approaches, and skills of professionals with different backgrounds. If you want to influence policy, make a difference or create new opportunities within a local community, develop innovative products, and more, you may find that working outside of university structures offers more direct and impactful ways of doing so.

The ways that your research and teaching skills prepare you for different kinds of careers, and the importance of creating meaningful connections for lasting impact, are all things to emphasize in cover letters and interviews. Doing so is particularly important in careers that are further removed from the university context. If the employer isn't expecting to hire someone with a PhD, demonstrating the ways in which your studies have enabled you to build a strong foundation can be the difference between getting an interview and being overlooked.

Getting Started: Where to Begin?

One thing that commonly frustrates students is that there is not really a list of steps to take or job options to consider for those who hope to explore a wider range of future opportunities than what can be found within traditional department structures. Most programs lack even a straightforward list of where their alumni are working, aside (perhaps) from those who hold faculty positions. A more robust database of career outcomes would, of course, help with this—but, even then, such a database will more likely show broad patterns and kinds of pathways rather than a clear set of job titles that PhDs might consider since there is such a wide range of unique titles and opportunities.[3] Even beyond this particular issue, every individual set of circumstances, priorities, challenges, and skills differs, so there is simply no single set of instructions or advice that can universally apply to all humanities PhDs. With that challenge in mind, the practical suggestions that I have to offer for prospective, current, and recent graduate students are less of a how-to manual and more a set of principles to consider and work toward as you determine the path that is best for you.

For Prospective Graduate Students

If you are thinking through these questions before you begin a PhD, that's wonderful! For many students, the question of careers comes much later, and it is a harder nut to crack when the dissertation is nearly done. There are a number of questions to ask yourself as you consider potential PhD programs to ensure that you're stepping into a program that will open as many doors as possible.

→ *Intellectual opportunities.* First, make sure that the program is a good fit in terms of your desired area of study and faculty members with whom you hope to work. (Do keep in mind, though, that these can and likely will shift over time, and faculty members may leave.)

→ *Money.* Consider the size of the program and the funding they offer. Will you have to take out loans? I strongly recommend you only pursue programs that will offer you a livable amount of support rather than going into debt for the program. Because everyone's needs are different depending on outside support and obligations, you might consider speaking with a financial counselor to ensure you are making a decision that will work for you.

→ *Signs of success.* Apply a critical lens to the program's website. Do they list "job placements" for recent graduates? If so, what do they mean by that? If the site celebrates more than just faculty positions, that is a good sign that broader career pursuits will be encouraged and supported.

→ *Support.* Talk to current students. What kind of support do they receive outside of the formal, curricular aspects of the program? If things like workshops, skillshare sessions, opportunities for feedback, professional development/travel funding, and formal and informal mentorship are in place, those are all good signs. Look for programming run by the department, self-organized by the students, or offered by the graduate school, library, or humanities center (if your institution has one). Having a structure in place to foster a supportive community will likely go a long way toward your well-being.

→ *Broad connections.* Investigate whether the program has any formal or informal connections across the campus or outside the academy. Do they routinely bring in speakers from nearby cultural heritage organizations, or partner with your university's library or humanities center on projects? What about local companies or community-based organizations? That kind of cross-cutting work is generally a strong indication of openness and of the way the program values engagement beyond its own walls.

→ *Openness to innovative scholarship.* If you are interested in pursuing modes of scholarship that are not currently standard, talk with faculty and students about how open the program is to projects that push the boundaries. What are the program's (and the graduate school's) policies related to dissertations? What kinds of scholarly work are faculty members doing? If you sense that doing the kind of work you want to do will be an uphill battle all the way, you may be setting yourself up for a long and painful journey.

For Current Graduate Students

If you are like many graduate students in the humanities, you may have begun your studies with the expectation that you would pursue a faculty career after completing your degree. Perhaps you are beginning to consider other options as the end of your doctoral program grows near. Or maybe your research itself has taken your career interests in a different direction than you anticipated. In either case, you may find that your program is not structured in a way to help you achieve your goals. If you are midway through your studies, there are a number of things that you can do to make the most of your current program, even if you are discovering that there are things you wish were a bit different.

→ *Get involved.* Are there opportunities your program offers that you have not taken advantage of? Even if you feel extremely busy, devote one semester to trying to say "yes" more frequently so that you can get a better sense of which elements may be most useful to you without derailing your progress toward the degree. Sometimes seemingly one-off opportunities open surprising doors that become central for your future. Going to events, joining a committee, contributing to community building within your department—all of these can be great ways to meet contacts, develop skills, and assess your interests.

→ *Find support.* If your program doesn't offer much by way of training or support, take a look at adjacent programs, the broader graduate school in which your program is housed, and cocurricular/extracurricular opportunities. There may be workshops or writing groups that can help you to find what you need outside your department.

→ *Build your skills.* If you are looking to hone a particular skill and can't find a way to do it within your program, consider an intensive short-term training opportunity such as the Digital Humanities Summer Institutes, Humanities Intensive Learning and Teaching, or the Digital Pedagogy Lab.[4] (There are many others with different areas of focus.) These can be pricey, but they often offer steeply discounted prices (and sometimes full scholarships) for current students. You might also consider seeking a part-time job or volunteer opportunity that will enable you to learn something new in an area that matters to you.

→ *Look to professional organizations.* In addition, many groups have been hosting shorter workshops immediately before or after major professional conferences, such as the Modern Language Association, the American Studies Association, and HASTAC. If you're going to one of these conferences anyway, it may be worth it to add an extra day to your trip. (Various factors, including family obligations, work commitments, and finances can make such off-site opportunities inaccessible. If that is the case for you, focus on local possibilities and online resources, which many of these conferences and workshops now offer. Don't sacrifice your health or well-being.)

→ *Push for improvements.* If you're feeling dissatisfied with particular aspects of your program and you have ideas for possible solutions, pitch them in a professional and well-researched way. Your department may or may not be able to offer you the change you seek, but it can be worth it to ask—not only for your own sake, but for the sake of your peers and future students in the program as well. If nothing else, it's a good professional skill to hone—how to ask for something in a way that centers on the work and what the change will afford rather than the negative aspects of what isn't working for you.

For Everyone

No matter what stage of your studies—or career—you are in, there are many things that you can do to position yourself to find a career path that is meaningful, that draws on your strengths and knowledge, and where you can grow and thrive.

Get to Know People

Regardless of what path you ultimately pursue, you can strengthen your footing by getting to know people in positions and fields that interest you. It is perhaps the single most important way that you can set yourself up for successful outcomes in your career searches. There are many ways that you can organically expand your circle of connections—even if you think of yourself as an introvert.

→ *Seek out stories and models that you find inspiring.* Even if you are not on the job market yet—in fact, *especially* if you are not on the job market yet—it is a great idea to take note of individuals or particular jobs that sound great to you. See a job ad that sounds perfect? Jot down what about it is appealing. Over time, you will likely see patterns that will help you make smart decisions in the jobs you seek.

→ *Listen in on different conversations.* Especially if you are trying to break into a new industry, you need to spend some time familiarizing yourself with the way that industry works, how it talks about different topics, and how it understands itself. Think of yourself as an ethnographer gleaning insights about a particular group of subjects. What are the questions that people working in the field are grappling with? What are the norms and assumptions? What vocabulary do they use? How formal do they tend to be? What irritates them? Of course, all of this will vary a bit by individual, but there are powerful patterns that you can tap into by listening. The reason this is so important is that it gives you a major edge once it's time to apply and interview for a position—and really even when you feel ready to introduce yourself to someone in the field. You will be more likely to use terminology that leaves people nodding their heads along with you, sensing that you "get" it—and far less likely to say something that inadvertently marks you as an outsider. You'll be more likely to ask smart questions and to raise issues that the person has also been thinking about. It's a way of building some trust and credibility in a field where you may not have direct experience.

Online communities are powerful resources for this. Spend some time on Twitter following people in the field that piques your interest. You may not feel ready to say anything; that's fine. Just take some time to read and listen, and apply your close reading skills to what people are saying. It will give you a huge leg up when you're ready to take the next step.

→ *Meet as many people as you can.* As you listen and grow more comfortable in the environments where you hope to make connections, start speaking up and letting people get to know you. Sometimes people tense up when they hear the word "networking"; if that's the case for you, then find another word. It doesn't matter what you call it; what matters is that you push yourself to encounter different people, listen to them, and talk to them. This can happen in many different ways. Take a moment to introduce yourself to a speaker after she gives a talk. Say hello to the people sitting around you in the audience at that talk. Talk to people at conferences. Respond to people on Twitter. Join Slack teams on topics you're interested in. Explore meetup.org and go to meet-ups in your area. Volunteer for something you care about. Not every connection has to have an immediately clear purpose—people can tell when a discussion is "transactional," for one thing, and will be less likely to open up. Find ways that you can be helpful to others; that will make the experience feel much more organic and less self-serving. It is also impossible to know who or what might become useful or important down the road. You never know who might find themselves in a position to hire or recommend someone in a month or a year, or who might see a job opportunity cross their desk, and if your name and face come to mind, you may find that they reach out to you. I know that I have done that when I see job ads that strike me as relevant for someone I have met or someone I know well. And, of course, recommendations that come via word of mouth from a trusted source are hugely valuable to hiring managers.

Know the Terrain

It's important to know the terrain within your program, across your academic field more broadly, and in potential areas of career interest.

→ *Learn what resources are available to you and seek out others.* Start within your own university. Larger institutions may have career resource centers devoted specifically to graduate students, often directed by someone who also holds a PhD and who deeply understands the decisions that graduate students face and the options available to you. Other institutions may have someone who focuses on graduate student needs working within a more generalized career center, or perhaps someone working within the graduate school who focuses on careers and professional development. If your university has a person—or an entire office—dedicated to this kind of service, it will be your number-one resource for up-to-date information and resources related to job opportunities and job search preparation.

If you do not have access to such an office, seek out more generalized resources. The Graduate Career Consortium is an association for graduate-student-focused career offices, and their website contains a section of student resources. Explore relevant hashtags on Twitter, like #altac, #withaphd, and more, which offer a dynamic space for resources and discussions related to career paths. As you explore, be skeptical of any advice that claims to have students' best interest in mind yet categorically undervalues a particular path, that seems to shame people who pursue one particular option, or that monetizes people's fears and anxieties.

→ *Aim high and be prepared to work.* In my experience, PhDs have a tendency to simultaneously under- and overvalue their skills. It's important to find a balance between the two, while still keeping an intention to aim high. For instance, it is worth remembering that even if you stick to a faculty path, an assistant professorship is a tough starting point that requires many years of intense work toward tenure and promotion. If you are breaking into a new industry, you can absolutely expect to do some hard work as you get up to speed and prove yourself in the field. At the same time, you have incredibly valuable skills and you should be careful not to undervalue them. If it's your first position and you are looking at roles that require only a bachelor's degree, look for something that also requires specialized skills that you have, or that offers clear pathways for advancement. Try to find ways that you can see your studies as experience that qualifies you for a particular job, even if it's not quite the kind of experience that the people writing the ad may have expected. One important reminder: you, not the prospective employer, will need to do the work of translating your experience and making it legible, especially if it falls outside the usual norms. But you can absolutely do that! Don't expect people to immediately understand why your graduate training is valuable, but don't undercut it, either.

→ *Recognize the signal value of your credential—and potential biases against it too.* Depending on the kind of position you are looking for, the PhD itself may carry important weight, independent from all you have learned in your particular content area. If you are looking for positions where you will be working with faculty members or universities in any capacity, the PhD offers a signal that you understand the values, environment, and challenges of their work—and it may therefore be easier to gain trust and respect. At the same time, if you're looking into environments where doctoral-level education is not the norm, know that at times you may need to work against biases to convince potential employers and colleagues that you understand and are ready for the kind of work the job entails. This sentiment was expressed when I interviewed employers who hire people with PhDs. Louis Pitschmann, dean of libraries at the University of Alabama, phrased it this way: "Many employers with whom I have spoken over the past thirty-five years express concern that a person with a PhD may not work as hard and contribute any more than a person doing the same job but without the PhD. Some employers worry that a person with a PhD will look down on colleagues and superiors who do not hold the PhD."[5] As in the previous point, a balance of confidence and humility is important.

→ *Make your academic work meaningful to you.* Even if your courses are structured in a traditional way, think about ways that you can envision your work reaching a broader audience than only your professor. Creating public-facing work can be one way of making connections and having an impact that extends far beyond the usual reach of formal educational structures. This can take different forms depending on your field; perhaps your research has elements that could be implemented through a community-based organization, or shared with local leaders to suggest policy recommendations. You might stage a performance or creative installation, or pitch an element of your work to a more generalized publication like *Slate* or the *Atlantic*. Or perhaps you can simply publish your work on a blog, sharing it with others across social media and relevant networks. Networks like HASTAC or Humanities Commons that specifically cater to scholars and teachers (and that won't sell your data) can give you a jump-start in building an audience, making them especially productive as you begin to share your work. Any of those modes takes your scholarship out of the narrow bounds of single readership and into a broader conversation with others.

→ *Be aware of your own material needs.* This is an important one. What are the baseline requirements that you need in order to have a healthy and happy life? These variables are intensely personal, and you need to figure out what is right for you. For some, location is crucial. You may be trying to stay in a particular geographic area for personal reasons; you may have a partner whose professional pathway also needs to be considered; you may have kids, or be caring for a parent, or have any number of things that make it hard to relocate. Then again, this may not be an important factor for you; maybe you're open to new locations and wouldn't mind trying somewhere new. Same with salary and benefits; you need to figure out what is a requirement for you, and where you can flex. And there may be intangibles that are important to you— things like work environment, flexibility, travel requirements, professional development opportunities, and more. You may not be able to find a job that checks every box, but make a conscious decision about whether something is worth fighting for or if you can let it go.

→ *Don't shortchange your intellectual needs and desires.* Will a certain position be stimulating (or at least open up future pathways that will become more stimulating)? Do you need to keep up some kind of activity in your subject area in order to feel satisfied, or can you find ways to be curious and creative in many different topic areas? If you absolutely need to keep some research going in your area of study, are there ways you can negotiate for that if it isn't built into the job you're considering? Sometimes you can negotiate for some research time—or at least some travel funding, even if research has to be done on your own time. But it's also worth noting that you may not need to stay wedded to your subject area. You may find that you love exploring new areas, and that you feel comfortable moving into new fields, even if it means you don't stay up-to-date in your field of study.

Focus on What Matters

While I'm highly skeptical of rhetoric that encourages people to "do what you love"—since "love" can easily be manipulated to substitute for wages, benefits, and decent work conditions, as I discuss in chapter 1—I do think that articulating what matters to you is an important step. You could think of this as a recurring practice. Each time you complete a project, scan a job ad, or consider a new opportunity, take a moment to jot down what feels meaningful or appealing about it. If you find yourself bristling against something, jot that down, too. Having a rough list of values, the kinds of work that you enjoy doing, things you absolutely hate, and more can help you find patterns that may lead you to uncover different career ideas than you otherwise might. Moreover, the act of reflecting in this way can help you to refine your scholarly work so that it is meaningful to you and advances your goals. Even if you do hope to work in a faculty career, self-reflection may help you to determine the kinds of institutions and positions that would be the best fit. If you absolutely love classroom teaching, you might look at community colleges or small liberal-arts colleges, for instance, and you might try forging deeper connections between your research and pedagogy. It can also be incredibly helpful to reflect on what you dislike doing or tend to subconsciously avoid.

All of these suggestions can be thought of as guiding principles that help you to frame your own search. If you're reading this early in your graduate studies, that is a huge advantage; the way you think about your future opportunities may have a significant impact on the way you approach your research and teaching. While it is essential to begin thinking about your career options as early as possible in your studies, that doesn't mean that you need to make a decision about the path you will choose. Consider ways that you can open new possibilities for your future self, all while strengthening your graduate work.

Eventually, as you get to know the field, expand your network, and continue developing your skills and interests, you will begin finding opportunities that really excite you. Like the academic job market, most searches are relatively opaque and it can be difficult to find the information you need in order to present yourself at your best and make an informed decision about the opportunity. That said, the process of applying, interviewing, negotiating your offer, and getting your footing in a new role can be challenging, but also incredibly rewarding.

The Search Process: Resources and Suggestions

There are many career-related resources that can help you to move through the process. I highly recommend connecting with your university's career resource office, especially if they have staff specifically focused on graduate students; they will have up-to-date information, sample materials, and assessments that you can use as starting points for your career exploration.[6] Books and guides that address the job search process are myriad, and even those that are not targeted to your exact situation can be incredibly valuable in helping to lay bare some of the tacit knowledge that can be the difference between getting an interview or being overlooked.

Numerous websites offer concrete and personalized support; I especially recommend those that are created by nonprofit professional associations and are available free to students and jobseekers. One such resource is Imagine PhD, a free and confidential website launched by the Graduate Career Consortium.[7] This site offers a robust set of personal assessments, individual stories, resources (including sample job application materials), and the opportunity to create a personal plan with customized goals. Focusing primarily on people in the humanities and social sciences, the website groups positions into several major job families that users can explore based on interest and skills. These categories include some positions squarely within higher education—faculty, higher education administrators—as well as areas such as advocacy, consulting, communications, organizational management, human services, research, and more.

Another valuable resource is the MLA's Doctoral Student Career Planning Guide, developed as part of the Connected Academics program.[8] The resources on this site are static, rather than customized to the user, but they are a robust framework for approaching a broad career search within the academy. With sections on concrete skills, like résumé writing, as well as high-level topics like sustainability in humanities programs, the website can also support faculty mentors in the guidance they offer to students and in pushing for reform within their home institutions. The concluding module offers a packet of activities including self-assessments and job ad analyses, as well as suggestions for creating a job search plan. These and other resources are the best ways to find up-to-date guidance, self-assessments, sample application materials, ideas for how to begin exploring new possibilities, and much more.

Search Process, Materials, and Timing

Job searches outside the academy differ significantly from the faculty job search process that many have been socialized to consider the norm. Faculty job searches follow a relatively standard (and lengthy) timetable: announcements typically go up in the fall, initial interviews take place in winter (often at conferences), and campus visits and offers move forward in spring. This is not the case for most other kinds of job opportunities, which generally open when a position becomes available and close as soon as it has been filled. For jobs that are embedded in the universe of higher education, you may find the search process to be somewhere in between, as position start dates may be tied to late summer or the beginning of the academic calendar. Even if the positions follow an academic calendar, though, the search timeline is likely to be condensed, so you may not see open positions until two to three months before the start date.

Next, the tricky part: where should you look for these jobs? Unlike faculty positions, there is simply no ready-made list of potential jobs or employers for humanities PhDs. The job titles are varied and resources for the search are ever changing. Instead, use your research skills to find opportunities. Start your search the way you might start searching for research materials in a new subject area. Maybe you have a few nonnegotiables, like location or salary (more on that in a moment). Maybe you think you'd really like to work in a particular industry. Start searching a broad jobs database (like indeed.com or LinkedIn) or databases that are slightly more targeted (like Higher Ed Jobs, jobs.gov, or idealist.org) and see what you pull up using terms that are relevant to what you're looking for.

Don't get hung up on what you think you should be looking for, or be overly rigid about your search; this first step is an exercise with no stakes, so search for anything that seems even faintly interesting as you begin. You might try industry-related terms as general as "nonprofit," "education," or "language." Talk to someone in the field to get other ideas about what to look for—another reason networking is incredibly helpful. Searches for specific job titles can also be valuable. What is meant by "coordinator," "specialist," or "director" in different contexts? Skills can be another good way to search. What kinds of jobs do you find when you search under "research," "writing," "analysis," or "translation"? Think of this as the "shitty first draft" stage of your job search.[9] Then, drill deeper into the postings that spark your interest. Don't worry too much if there are deal breakers in the postings at this stage, or if you feel wildly under- or overqualified. Start by noticing patterns in the links you're clicking. Do they all emphasize a particular skill? Do they have a particular type of work environment? Focus on a particular subject area? Once you can see patterns, look back at the job ads and focus on other keywords. Then, use those keywords to search more deeply and uncover other opportunities that the first broad search may not have uncovered. The search process will be iterative—you can expect to toggle between broad searches and more targeted ones many times, flagging only the most promising to pursue.

The materials required upon application are also different for faculty positions than for most other kinds of job searches. Rather than a dossier with a personal statement, teaching philosophy, sample syllabi, writing sample, reference letters, and more, you will most likely submit only a cover letter and CV or résumé, both of which should be tailored to each job you apply for. Cover letters should also be shorter than what you might write for a faculty position. If a job ad doesn't make clear exactly what materials are expected, make sure to ask—and do not send any unsolicited materials. Adding a writing sample when none is requested will not endear you to hiring managers. It is better to ask than to assume and send the wrong thing.

Above all, all of your materials should be crafted to show how you can meet the prospective employer's needs. Rather than narrate what is already visible in your CV, your cover letter should make explicit connections to what the employer is seeking. Some sections on your CV should likely be reordered and expanded or contracted so that the most important information is foregrounded. For instance, you may want to start with relevant experience, and move an abbreviated teaching section toward the end. You might also need to pare down your list of publications or presentations, which can be a little bit painful to do. If a résumé is requested, you'll need to cut all but the most important information from your CV, and frame it in a way that connects with the specific position you're applying for—down to mirroring the language used in the job ad.

Every organization approaches the interview process slightly differently. You will most likely have at least two interviews, with at minimum the hiring manager and a human resources representative, but this can vary. Most importantly, make sure to prepare as deeply as possible for each interview, learning the work of the people you'll be meeting with, the organization's mission and points of pride, and major questions in the field.

Finally, there are a few elements to the interview process that may seem minor or even unnecessary, but can mean the difference between getting a job or not. First, you should always be prepared to ask one or two substantive questions at the end of each interview—this is a chance for prospective employers to gauge your interest and engagement. It's a moment for you to show that you've done your research, that you have a handle on the role and what its challenges would be, and that you understand the key issues animating the organization or field where you're seeking a position. It's also a good idea to ask briefly about next steps and timing so that you can set your expectations accordingly. However, the interview is not the time to ask about details like salary or benefits; that happens later, during the negotiation stage (which I discuss below).

Last but not least, etiquette matters—a lot. The interview begins with the very first encounter you have with anyone at the organization, via email or in person, so be courteous, professional, and kind to every single person you interact with. Be on time, dress well, greet everyone in the room with a handshake, and email a thank-you note to everyone on the committee after the interview. The thank-you note in particular is often a missed opportunity; much like asking good questions at the end of an interview, a postinterview email is a chance to reiterate your interest, underscore or amplify something that you may have said during the interview that you think is especially important, or make note of something one of the interviewers said that struck a chord with you and that you have been reflecting on since the conversation. While the practice of sending thank-you notes varies by industry, I have never heard of a case where someone reacted negatively to receiving one. Above all, remember through the entire process that you're engaging with prospective colleagues—people with whom you would potentially spend a huge amount of time, day after day. The job search process can feel dehumanizing at times, but the more human and present you can be, the more likely it is that the search committee will feel that you can not only do the job but that you're also someone with whom they would like to work.

Salary and Negotiation

As you refine your choices, make sure to research not only the content and context of the job—that is, the type of work, the institution, the people with whom you would work—but also the economic and material realities of the position. You can do some of this without having to talk with anyone directly. Before going into an interview, you should have at least a rough guess of what a reasonable salary range might be (if the job ad doesn't provide one). Commercial tools can be useful for this—Glassdoor and Indeed both offer good baselines for salary information. If you're applying to a nonprofit or publicly funded institution, it should be possible to find precise salary information based on required reporting. Nonprofits are required to file a tax form called a 990 (or a 990-PF), which will be made available on the organization's website or through GuideStar, a source of information on nonprofits and charitable organizations. At minimum, the five highest salaries will be made available, which you can use to calibrate your expectations. (If the executive director earns $80,000 per year, don't go into an interview for a junior position and expect to receive the same amount.) Public institutions, like state universities, must also publicly disclose salaries. How you view this information varies state by state, and in some cases the information is available but difficult to navigate or interpret. Even if that is the case, having some sense of what is reasonable will be an immense help going into the interview (and even before, in determining whether to pursue the position).

Salary information can help ensure that you neither overvalue nor undervalue your worth, both of which can be damaging in the interview process. If you have never earned more than a graduate student stipend, know that a full-time salary for a PhD holder should (thankfully) be far higher, even in an entry-level position. At the opposite end of the spectrum, do keep in mind that, especially if you don't have a wealth of work experience yet, it will take time to work your way into senior positions.

The first salary is important because it becomes the baseline against which future earnings will be measured. Some positions may ask you what you earned in prior positions and may calibrate their offer accordingly. (This practice exacerbates wage inequality for women, people of color, and others in underrepresented identity categories, and is fortunately starting to be phased out. The state of Massachusetts banned the practice in 2016 in an explicit effort to improve pay equity,[10] and a handful of other locations have followed suit, including California, Delaware, Oregon, New York City, Philadelphia, and Puerto Rico.[11] While a nationwide ban has been proposed, many places—including many public institutions—still require such disclosure as a condition of employment.) Moreover, any raises that you receive within a single institution will be based on that first salary, so it's important not to settle for something that is lower than it should be. Because wages are such a delicate subject, it is likely that your only source of information will be what you can glean online.

This brings up the question of negotiating your job offer. First, especially for people who are not white men, I think it is absolutely essential to negotiate.

An employer's initial offer is probably going to be lower than what is possible, and even if it isn't, it is structurally important to ensure that you are earning the maximum amount the organization is willing to offer. As a woman, I have made it a principle to negotiate every job offer I receive, if for no other reason than the fact that men typically negotiate while women often do not, and this alone contributes to gendered wage inequality. As someone who is averse to conflict and who finds these conversations uncomfortable, I have tried to de-center myself and think of the structural implications when asking if an institution can offer anything more. Do your research and consider suggesting a number, noting that based on your research, someone with your level of education and experience earns approximately that amount in that field.

When negotiating, be concrete and reasonable, and consider more than just money. Asking for a higher base wage is a good starting point, but do be sure that your request is reasonable. The background research you have done will be helpful in this, and it is generally acceptable to ask for 10 percent higher than the initial offer. But don't limit yourself to that alone. What are some other tangible or intangible things that would greatly increase the desirability of the position for you? Some things to consider are flexible work arrangements (including flexible schedules and remote work), professional development (research or travel funds, money for courses or books), relocation support, and dedicated research time.

When framing these requests, do so not only in terms of how they will benefit you as an individual but also how they will make the position more valuable and strengthen what you can do for the institution. For instance, dedicated research time can bring not only prestige through publications and academic standing but also may spark unexpected developments that become directly useful to the institution. Google famously offered 20 percent research time to its employees not only to increase worker satisfaction, but for profit-driven reasons as well: some of the ideas generated during that research time led to creative new product development, including the development of Gmail and AdSense.[12] All this is to say that you don't need to feel selfish for asking for the conditions that will enable you to do your best work.

You may feel concerned that asking for more will put your offer at risk. But if the institution has reached the point where they are offering you a position, they really want you and are unlikely to rescind their offer on the basis of a reasonable negotiation request. This is an expected part of the offering process at many (or most) institutions. Of course, it is a delicate process and one that you want to approach with care, respect, and ample information, as there have occasionally been stories of rescinded offers.[13] But as long as you are making requests that are within the bounds of reason, and doing so in a respectful and positive way—trying to reach an outcome that is desirable for both you and the institution—you have nothing to fear. Throughout it all, be human and show your enthusiasm for the position. The goal is not to convey a sense of dissatisfaction, but to show excitement and a desire to reach a mutually satisfactory outcome so that you can join the team.

If there is one guiding principle to take away from all of this, it is this: research your job prospects, know your own needs, and consider the search to be the opportunity to bring these two threads together. The search for a job that feels right is not so much a matter of finding one perfect piece to fit a complex puzzle, but rather a chance to explore what possibilities might stretch you in new ways, all while keeping your own constraints in mind.

Career Goals and the Dissertation

If you're not quite at the stage to begin your job search, you may be wondering whether and how to tailor your studies in such a way that they prepare you to be a competitive candidate in a range of career fields. In some ways, this is a problematic approach; your scholarly work itself will probably not be the sole thing that lands you a job outside a faculty career, and you may shortchange your academic trajectory in the process, or find yourself working on a topic in which you're not really invested. At the same time, depending on your interests, there are ways that you can approach your work in an exploratory way that can help you to make connections and build the kinds of translatable skills that will help you to feel equipped to take whatever next step you choose. In many cases, the dissertation proposal is the best moment to undertake such an approach. If you have a supportive advisor and committee who will have your back if your approach is questioned, the autonomous and extended nature of the dissertation can be a perfect moment to create a project that is meaningful to you and your future aspirations.

For students considering careers beyond the classroom, the traditional model of the dissertation may feel limiting. Depending on your goals and your research interests, you may wonder about ways that you can demonstrate the ability to conduct thorough research and articulate a sustained argument that deviate from the protomonograph model of most humanities dissertations. Breaking out of the traditional formats of scholarly work can be challenging—not only for doctoral students, but for faculty members as well. I explore the challenges and opportunities of innovative scholarly publishing, including digital and nontraditional dissertation formats, in chapter 3. It may not be an easy road, but if your research questions present clear needs and opportunities for exploring different forms and structures for your work, then you might consider doing something new in order to craft a project that is structurally aligned with the new insights you hope to share. Doing so, however, is indeed risky. As a student, you are vulnerable. If you want to undertake something that does not clearly fit into the rubrics that your program or university have set up for degree attainment, you must ensure that you have the strong, vocal support of your advisor (and preferably your entire committee). Even if you have that support, you should prepare to do some extra legwork to document the ways in which your project satisfies the requirements for a dissertation, as well as translational work to make your project legible to skeptics. If you are prepared to take this on, you may end up creating an incredible project, and you will almost certainly be better prepared to articulate its value and unique contribution than someone writing a standard dissertation who has not had to defend its structure as well as its content.

If you are considering whether to tackle a unique project as a dissertation, I highly recommend spending time not only with examples of creative dissertations, but also (and especially) with material that reflects on or provides documentation of the processes so that you can anticipate surprises that may await. In chapter 3, I shared the example of Amanda Visconti's digital dissertation project, "Infinite *Ulysses*." Beyond the project itself, Visconti also went further, engaging in a crucial meta-analysis of her own project by blogging every stage of her research, development, and defense. When I asked her about what she found most important about that experience, Visconti emphasized that her project helped her to see the value of experimentation, mentorship, community, and documentation—not only the value of these elements *to* scholarship, but their value *as* scholarship. Doing metalevel analysis of her own work gave her a clearer vision for each of the choices she made:

> Getting to do an unusually shaped dissertation meant doing a lot of meta-dissertational work analyzing and synthesizing precedents for making as scholarship, dissertations that didn't focus on chapters, and experimental methods and formats in general. I not only needed to prove that such work could reach the goals of a dissertation, but that it also fit the goals of my particular areas of research. It was profoundly useful to work through what I thought, and then convince others as well. . . . It strikes me as unfortunate that most humanities dissertation creators aren't supported in arguing for why their format is the best one for their research questions, rather than treating written chapters as the obvious choice.[14]

Visconti's work of documentation and reflection is a tremendous contribution to the community, as it helps to make transparent the hurdles (and successes) that other emerging scholars might anticipate when working on digital projects. Because a creative dissertation project is often the only one of its kind within a program, the fact that Visconti made this body of work publicly available rather than letting it become part of the tacit knowledge shared only with her committee is incredibly valuable. Most importantly, since policies and practices vary across programs and universities, Visconti has created signposts that other junior scholars can reference as examples of successful projects—a huge asset to someone doing a new kind of work.

Along with other formal requirements like comprehensive exams (and sometimes methods courses), dissertations are an area where structural interventions can have a profound effect on the nature of a graduate program. There are certainly ways that individuals can craft their own projects to meet their research needs, but how far a student can deviate from the standard structure varies widely by institution and remains largely idiosyncratic. Given that, it forms a pivot point between individual opportunity and the need for institutional change. Students can do a great deal to make the most of their graduate program and shape their training to meet their needs, but at a certain point it is the structures themselves that must be reevaluated. Doing so also strengthens the possibilities for student learning, since remaining open to a wider range of potential outcomes is necessary for engaged, student-centered learning. It simply does not make sense to open up a creative process while remaining wedded to singular outcomes in terms of scholarly work products and eventual career paths. Given greater possibility and agency, it is to be expected that students will move in different directions as they imagine new applications and connections for their work.

As the capstone of doctoral training, the dissertation is the pivotal moment when graduate students synthesize and articulate their research, marking the transition from apprentice to scholar. It also serves an important professionalization and normative function: graduate students learn what is accepted as scholarly work based on the submission requirements for their dissertation and the values of their committee. For all of these reasons and more, the framework of what constitutes an acceptable—or an outstanding—dissertation is a powerful marker of what is happening within a given field. Changing what constitutes a successful dissertation has the potential to change a great deal about graduate programs, from start to finish in a student's tenure: what programs look for in prospective students, how they structure coursework and exam requirements, and what kinds of careers graduates pursue.

In fact, the question is also important for students who do hope to pursue faculty positions. The landscape of scholarly communication is changing, and while peer-reviewed journals and monographs still dominate the field, it is increasingly common to see meaningful research happening in nontraditional spaces. As scholarly communication changes, the dissertation naturally follows suit. Digital platforms are a part of this, and indeed much of the discussion about new forms of the dissertation has centered around digital dissertations.

Digital work is an increasingly important element of the dissertation and of academic work in general. There is a wide range of what this can include, and certainly a basic level of digital engagement and literacy are required for any research project. Personal blogs are commonplace (and, in some cases, even passé), and multimodal publishing options, such as Scalar, are increasingly popular. In more sophisticated projects, students can effectively become not only the lead researcher but also the project manager for a dissertation, determining the scope of the project, the tools used, and the desired final product and audience. They set timelines and engage collaborators for areas outside their skill sets. The research itself is still the most vital skill, along with articulating that research through a written argument, but the ancillary work of bringing the project to fruition can be easily translated into a wide range of professional environments, both within university structures and beyond them.

But this is only a small piece of a broader consideration of the form and purpose of the dissertation specifically and research more generally. If nonstandard modalities engage students in sustained research and the composition of a clear, compelling argument while also bringing new insight to publics beyond the dissertation committee, then the capstone project can potentially have a far more significant impact than a standard dissertation might, as I discussed in chapter 3. Further, celebrating the scholarly merit of new kinds of projects also means that students will be primed to succeed in more varied career paths. Innovative projects may require specific skills—like video editing, web development, or database design—and they will undoubtedly require more generalized skills such as project management, navigating institutional hurdles, and public engagement. For some, finding avenues for innovative scholarly work is a key aspect of preparing for multiple career possibilities.

Returning to the broad goals of this chapter, I hope that students feel better equipped to see the elements of doctoral study not so much as steps leading in a single direction, but rather as building blocks that can be assembled in many different configurations—and I hope faculty feel prepared to support students

CHAPTER FIVE

in discerning and achieving their goals. In many ways, the change in mind-set from a faculty-first career goal to a more expansive idea of what a fulfilling professional pathway might look like is the key first step. The process involves a great deal of translational work, in learning both to see and to articulate the ways that elements of the PhD—such as coursework, independent research, teaching, and leadership or service opportunities—are also highly valuable in a wide range of other contexts. In addition, envisioning a broader range of future possibilities may generate new and interesting research avenues as you consider how your work could be valuable not only for its own sake but to inform policy, transform systems, engage communities, and much more. The world needs you.

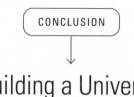

Building a University Worth Fighting For

This book began with an invitation, and ends with an injunction. Individual success stories about academic career diversity abound. And yet, despite decades of discussion, reform has still not permeated the institutional level, leaving assumptions about what constitutes scholarly success largely unchanged. It is time for all who are invested in higher education to take action—not to tear down the structures of the academy, but to reshape and strengthen them from within. At the Futures Initiative at the Graduate Center, CUNY, we have built this into our programming under the banner of the University Worth Fighting For. The underlying premise of this call is deeply optimistic: that such a university can exist, and that each action dedicated students, faculty, and administrators take can bring it one step closer to becoming a reality. This is the action to which I call readers now: to bring about a system of graduate education we can believe in, one step at a time.

In the preceding chapters, I have offered a diagnosis of the issues and analysis of obstacles and opportunities. Building on that foundation, I have offered suggestions for personal career advancement, as well as advising and mentorship. Throughout, I have proposed strategies for working toward broader graduate education reform, both long-term goals and concrete actions that can be implemented immediately. Key elements in moving toward systemic improvements include rethinking curricula with an eye toward collaboration and public engagement; tracking and celebrating the varied career outcomes of graduates; advocating for fair working conditions for all faculty members; and exploring ways to better support graduate students both during and after their studies. These actions serve everyone invested in higher education as a public good.

I am not the first person to recommend changes of this nature. There have been many efforts over the years to reform higher education so that it better supports student goals and connects more meaningfully to key societal issues. Looking back as far as 1837, the advent of Historically Black Colleges and Universities (HBCUs) offers one example of a systematic effort to provide not only education but also sites of empowerment and social change that enabled and encouraged students to make direct connections between their education and the world around them.[1] Change has been slower to come in predominantly white institutions, where in many cases professional norms still isolate rather than connect. The stickiness of the problem is partly due to the immense challenge of changing long-held but little-examined values, even when structures and programs change. As long as traditional markers of scholarly prestige (tenure, peer-reviewed journal articles, monographs) remain the coin of the realm in humanities disciplines, even the best interventions will likely have only a minimal or local impact.

Reimagining scholarly structures can begin simultaneously in grassroots and top-down ways. When students and recent graduates take steps toward their own professional fulfillment, and when prospective students increasingly seek programs that foster not only depth but breadth of thinking, programs have a stronger impetus to adopt new approaches and structures. And at the same time, when students enter new programs and are immediately encouraged to attend not only to academic rigor, but to application, engagement, accessibility, relevance, and translation as well, their work will take on tremendous potential for impact beyond the academy.

More than ever, we need people trained to read closely, articulate nuanced arguments, examine and interrogate assumptions, and understand the ways that values, meanings, and interpretations are culturally and contextually embedded. Humanities PhDs will continue to go into a wide range of careers no matter what, as they have long done. While I hope that this book has been helpful for individual students and scholars exploring their own pathways, the questions and issues at hand are even more pressing at the collective level. At the level of departments and institutions, the big questions are whether programs can be flexible and creative in finding ways to equip students for new possibilities; how innovative work with deep public relevance is evaluated and valued; and how programs can recognize and eventually adapt the values internalized in their recruitment and admissions practices.

As I have shown throughout the book, one of the most significant reasons that programs should be encouraging the pursuit of careers beyond the classroom is that of public impact, which reciprocally supports a reinvestment by the public in higher education. Thinking about career paths matters—not only to individuals who need jobs but also to disciplines and humanistic inquiry more broadly. Failing to recognize the ways that humanities graduate study is valuable in many different contexts will most likely lead to fewer scholars, fewer students in our classes, even less funding, and a downward spiral that devalues the humanities in general. If, instead, humanities scholars become more adept at drawing connections between their educational background, public interest, and employment opportunities, there is tremendous potential to engage the public more deeply and strengthen investment in the humanities. A deep humanistic education provides valuable insights into a world in which people are increasingly interconnected through social networks, the growing ease of communication and travel (for many), and the expansion of global industries. Equipping graduate students with new skills and literacies—from technical fluency to an understanding of organizational structures—not only prepares them for today's workplaces but is also critical to ensuring continued rigorous and creative research.

None of this is easy, but all of the intertwined topics and questions that I have addressed in this book point to the richness and innovation of work that we're seeing across many disciplines, as well as a changing set of opportunities and expectations. That's a good problem to have, even if there are difficult challenges to navigate as we collectively develop new practices, norms, and support structures. The best possible outcome would be a cultural shift that cultivates a deep appreciation of public engagement, supports meaningful careers that allow a healthy standard of living, and encourages diversity of all kinds in order to bring greater vibrancy to graduate study.

Doing this work will be a net good: for individuals, who can do groundbreaking work and gain valuable visibility and feedback from peers; for disciplines, as new knowledge emerges through new forms of scholarship and from the connections between the university and beyond it; and finally, but perhaps most importantly, for the public, which will have greater access to scholarly work and methods. If we truly consider higher education to be a public good, then it is time to recognize and celebrate the myriad ways that graduate study can strengthen and enrich the structures of our society.

Ten Ways to Begin

I hope that all readers feel inspired by the importance of career diversity in humanities PhD programs, and empowered to pursue the pathway that inspires them and support their students to do the same. As a final takeaway, here are ten suggestions for how to begin building a university that is truly worth fighting for, both at the individual and structural levels. Whether you are a student, faculty member, or administrator, there are things you can do right now.

1. Make space for exploration and reflection.

Graduate school can be all-encompassing. Despite—or perhaps because of—that, it is also deeply valuable to seek ways to stay connected with skills, interests, and communities that are not necessarily reflected in traditional academic work. Students, think about the things that energize you, that you're willing to make time for, that help you feel grounded; these can be useful indicators of what may one day become a fulfilling career path. Making space for priorities outside the university can bring greater perspective to your scholarly work. Consider developing a reflective practice in which you actively look for patterns among the areas of your life that build you up or that create stress, and allow those patterns to be signposts for possible future pathways.

Faculty members and administrators, you can make space for this kind of reflection by encouraging students to lead balanced lives. One way to do this is by asking questions—from the very earliest stages of graduate school—that make it clear that it is a good and normal thing to have commitments outside of the department. Ask open-ended questions and help students to see possible connections between their emerging scholarly interests and the things that motivate them in other ways. For instance, you might ask about how a student's research topic might be of use to a particular community group, or whether a student is involved in a relevant nonprofit. While talking about personal information can be delicate, sharing a bit about your own outside commitments can also be valuable. It can help students imagine their own futures if they know the professors they admire have lives outside the university as well.

2. Expand the notion of what constitutes meaningful scholarship—and how it can be evaluated.

Peer-reviewed journal articles and scholarly monographs are not the only way to share research—far from it. Graduate students and faculty members have many opportunities to push the boundaries of how to meaningfully share research (though the amount of risk an individual can take on varies widely). Students, it is important to find faculty who will support you if your dissertation falls outside your department's usual parameters, and be ready to point to examples of similar project. In addition, embrace flexibility with your approach; systems and requirements do not change overnight, and some measure of compromise might help you to avoid getting stuck.

If you are in a position to do so, help pave the way for more junior scholars to work creatively. Lobby for the acceptance of nontraditional dissertations that allow students to assemble and present their research in a way that makes sense for their future goals, and for the nature of their particular project. Train faculty in how to evaluate innovative work by drawing on tools developed by scholarly societies like the Modern Language Association. Support tenure cases for scholars who take risks, engage with different audiences, and connect with varied communities. Since prestige remains the coin of the realm for universities, finding ways to formally value public-oriented work and reintegrate that work into scholarly conversations is essential—both to reward scholars' work and to signal that creative applications of research are meaningful.

3. Build partnerships outside the university.

Which organizations and industries are important to the community where your institution is located? Consider finding ways to connect with them, either formally or informally. Think about public-oriented project ideas that align with your or your students' research interests and would also benefit a community-based organization. Rather than simply making the organization an object of study, invite them to join as collaborators and cocreators. From single projects, work toward longer partnerships that are mutually beneficial. Over time, these connections could evolve to offer internship opportunities, networks of knowledge and resources, and new ways of understanding the potential public impact of scholarly work.

As a corollary, be open to learning from many different sources—not just those that are formally academic in nature. Spending time listening to and learning from local communities, nonprofits, activist groups, journalists, and many, many others can give scholars a more balanced and grounded perspective on research. Building stronger public outreach and engagement also helps communities beyond the university to glimpse the work being done by researchers and teachers, and forges stronger respect and connection between the two.

4. Find small ways to incorporate professional development from the earliest days of the graduate school trajectory.

Professional development often comes too late, when expectations for a future trajectory are already set and anxieties are high. A better approach is to bring the topic into advising conversations, departmental events, and classrooms from day one. For instance, rather than evaluating students exclusively on their writing, develop collaborative project assignments that allow students to work together in a variety of roles and to communicate their findings to an array of audiences. Advisors might make a conscious effort to talk with students about past experiences and future plans. Help students develop translational ways of thinking about what they do in order to learn to reframe skills and interests for different contexts. And students, if you are not getting the support you need, ask for it—both individually and collectively with your peers.

5. Seek outside resources.

Sometimes the best resources may take a bit of digging to find, so students and faculty alike can apply their research skills in looking for support. Get to know the career center at your institution, especially if there are counselors who focus on graduate students. Explore online resources and toolkits from professional organizations. Investigate early so that you have ideas and resources ready at hand when you or your students need them.

Listen in on Twitter and in other informal online spaces. If you think you may need (or want) to develop a specific skill, like web design or a programming language, consider waiting to do a workshop or online tutorials until you have a project under way so that you have something concrete to work on as you learn. If possible, attend workshops and conferences in an area outside your usual field to build skills and develop a network. Sometimes different departments share different resources, so you might also consider organizing an interdisciplinary professional development meet-up with other graduate students at your institution to share suggestions, frustrations, and more.

6. Tune your program's curriculum to make the most of required courses.

If your program has required introductory or research methods courses as part of its curriculum, take a close look at the skills, values, and paradigms that it introduces to new students. Consider reshaping such courses to offer opportunities to students to think in a translational way about their program of study. Without sacrificing rigor or content, embedding the course in a broader context that reaches beyond the discipline and even beyond the academy can lead to deeper connections down the road. The course can be even more powerful if it adds a public-facing or collaborative project component, as students will begin to learn the power of working together toward a common goal that has a clear potential impact.

7. Recognize the importance of having good models.

Universities value innovative work, but they also stand on precedent and tradition. To support work that appears risky or unusual, students and administrators alike need to be able to point to others who have done similar work or pursued a similar path. Each graduate student who is hired into a high-level position or something with a great potential trajectory is one more person who can be a voice for the importance of higher education. But for that to be true, those pathways must be visible and celebrated.

To establish strong models within a department, consider reaching out to alumni and featuring their achievements and pathways on the department website; inviting speakers who represent a wider range of expertise and possible futures to help students gain ideas and build their networks; or building collaborations with like-minded programs at other institutions. Staying connected with and highlighting the work of former students is one of the simplest and least resource-intensive things that a program can do.

8. Work toward reform in multiple areas at once.

A thoughtful and comprehensive approach to reforming graduate education and equipping students for a wider range of professional paths requires consideration of questions related to the changing landscape of higher education. Issues such as labor practices, public investment in higher education, changes and opportunities in scholarly communication and digital pedagogy, and broad social justice issues such as racism and gender bias all affect the training that graduate students receive and the career paths they pursue. Strive to maintain awareness of the broader landscape of higher education and how issues in one area affect all other elements. All of these areas matter, but our energies are finite—so choose one thing that you care about and where you feel you can make a difference and start there. It is almost certainly connected to the broader aim of creating a healthy and sustainable educational system that is both rigorous and inclusive.

9. Work against racism, sexism, and other forms of bias in individual and systemic ways.

White scholars especially must learn to notice and work against systemic racism and sexism in our institutions and in the academy. Graduate students are under intense stress that can negatively affect physical and mental health, not to mention academic performance. This is even more true for students whose identities are historically underrepresented in the academy—women and nonbinary people of all races and ethnicities, people of color of all genders, first-generation students, LGBTQ+ people, and more. Advisors can be a first line of support and can help students to thrive, reach their goals, and pursue a career pathway of their choosing.

Critically examining problematic tendencies within a program is an important first step to developing a more fully inclusive institution that welcomes diverse backgrounds, varied perspectives, and new forms of knowledge. The systemic racism and widespread bias that make it more difficult for people from marginalized communities to thrive mean that faculty, students, and the public are generally learning from those who are in dominant cultural positions. To educate students in the fullest sense of the term, universities must become places where people from all backgrounds can question, challenge, explore, and articulate new views without fear of retribution.

10. Be a voice for change at the local level up to whatever is the biggest platform you can obtain.

Higher education needs your support, so join others in working toward meaningful reform. Try putting your research and writing skills to use in new ways that allow you to go beyond your research area to articulate the value of your work—and that of your colleagues—in a broader context. What has your education enabled you to do, and what difference does your research make in the world? Write op-eds that connect to current events or local issues. Go to conferences and give presentations not only on your research, but on structural issues that you care about. Use opportunities for speaking and writing to lift up the work of those around you. If you have a union, get involved so that you can get a sense of how your goals and concerns fit in with those of the broader institutional community. Speak up about departmental policies that may be problematic. Students, get involved in committees so that you can have a voice in the decisions that affect your trajectory. However you choose to get involved, and even if change is hard to see, know that your voice matters every step of the way. The time for change is now. Let's get started.

NOTES

Preface

1 Nowviskie, "#altac Origin Stories (with Tweets)."

2 Now, unfortunately, the term also calls to mind another use of the "alt" modifier—namely, "alt-right" as a euphemistic descriptor for white supremacist groups.

3 Many thanks to Andrew Sallans, William Corey, and Sherry Lake of the University of Virginia Library's Data Management Consulting Group, as well as research librarians Summer Durrant and Charles Kromkowski, all of whom offered valuable guidance throughout the research, analysis, and data deposit processes.

4 As of 2018, CUNY's enrollment includes about 250,000 degree-seeking students and another 250,000 who take courses but are not enrolled in degree programs.

5 Werner, "Make Your Own Luck."

Introduction: Putting the PhD to Work—for the Public Good

1 Main, Prenovitz, and Ehrenberg, "In Pursuit of a Tenure-Track Faculty Position," 22.

2 Laurence, "Where Are They Now?" The trend of low unemployment rates for advanced degree holders also holds true across other fields. In 2014, the unemployment rate for doctoral degree holders in all disciplines was just 2.1 percent, compared to a national average of 5.5 percent (Bureau of Labor Statistics, "Earnings and Unemployment Rates by Educational Attainment"). One missing element in this broad analysis is a more detailed and qualitative consideration of that work: for instance, to what extent do different kinds of positions offer a sense of intellectual engagement and professional accomplishment? What percentage of PhD holders earn at least a living wage and receive benefits? The data available in sources cited above as well as Humanities Indicators, the Integrated Postsecondary Education Data System (IPEDS), and the Survey of Earned Doctorates unfortunately do not provide this level of granularity. This lack is one more reason why it is so important for programs to track the professional trajectories of their alumni. In coming years, the Council of Graduate Schools' PhD Career Pathways surveys, in development at the time of writing, should also provide insight into these questions.

3 While the focus of this book is not primarily on labor issues, understanding the current landscape is crucial to making informed choices about graduate study. For a more sustained consideration of academic labor issues, see Bousquet, *How the University Works*; Cassuto, *The Graduate School Mess*; Newfield, *Unmaking the*

Public University; and Gupta, Habjan, and Tutek, *Academic Labour, Unemployment and Global Higher Education,* among others.

4   Among people receiving doctoral degrees in the humanities with definite employment commitments at the time of graduation, 76.4 percent were in academic positions. Survey of Earned Doctorates, "Doctorate Recipients from U.S. Universities 2016," table 46.

5   Rogers, "Humanities Unbound."

6   American Association of University Professors, "Here's the News: The Annual Report on the Economic Status of the Profession, 2012–13."

7   Jaschik, "Skepticism about Tenure, MOOCs, and the Presidency."

8   Woodrow Wilson National Fellowship Foundation, "The Responsive PhD: Innovations in U.S. Doctoral Education."

9   Modern Language Association, "Report of the Task Force on Doctoral Study in Modern Language and Literature."

10 For a darkly humorous example of how this plays out in libraries and scholarly publishing, see Nowviskie, "Fight Club Soap."

11 As of 2015, 56 percent of people with humanities PhDs held a primary job teaching at the postsecondary level. This number includes both tenure-track and non-tenure-track faculty positions. National Science Foundation, 2015 National Survey of College Graduates. Data analyzed and presented by the American Academy of Arts and Sciences' Humanities Indicators (http://www.humanities indicators.org).

12 Rogers, "Humanities Unbound."

13 Asked to identify the career(s) they expected to pursue when they started graduate school, 74 percent of respondents indicated that they expected to obtain positions as tenure-track professors. What is perhaps more interesting is these respondents' level of confidence: of the 74 percent anticipating a faculty career, 80 percent report feeling fairly certain or completely certain about that future path. This finding is corroborated by similar results in the 2017 working paper by Main, Prenovitz, and Ehrenberg, "In Pursuit of a Tenure-Track Faculty Position"; nearly all (96 percent) respondents in their sample initially pursued a faculty career after completing their PhD.

14 Respondents were reflecting on and reporting impressions they had prior to beginning their graduate study. The time span is broad, with entrance years for those who completed the PhD ranging from 1962 to 2008. While this range means that the results do not show a contemporary snapshot, they do give us a clear sense of the landscape over time. As such, it is clear that even among the body of people who are working in other roles, the dominant expectation at the outset of graduate school was for a future career as a professor.

15 Rogers, "Humanities Unbound."

16 Seltzer, Risam, and Applegate, "#MLA 2018."

17 Smith, *Manifesto for the Humanities,* 5.

Chapter 1: The Academic Workforce:
Expectations and Realities

1   Moten and Harney, "The University and the Undercommons"; Bérubé, "Presidential Address 2013"; Berens, "Digital Humanities 2013."

2   McCarty, "Getting There from Here."

3   Moten and Harney, "The University and the Undercommons," 102.

4   I will return to this idea in chapter 4 to propose that doctoral education must become generative, not reproductive.

5   American Association of University Professors, "Higher Education at a Crossroads: The Annual Report on the Economic Status of the Profession, 2015–16," 13.

6   National Labor Relations Board, "Board: Student Assistants Covered by the NLRA."

7   Coalition on the Academic Workforce, "A Portrait of Part-Time Faculty Members," tables 14 and 15. This figure is often used to justify the continued reliance on adjunct labor; however, there may be mitigating factors unrelated to professional goals that affect people's relative desire to pursue full-time work. For instance, it is possible that many of the adjuncts who prefer part-time employment are parents who are expected to be the primary caregiver in their household and for whom more viable employment options are not available.

8   June and Newman, "Adjunct Project Reveals Wide Range in Pay."

9   Modern Language Association, "MLA Recommendation on Minimum Per-Course Compensation for Part-Time Faculty Members."

10   Reed, "Classic College Movies Updated for the Adjunct Era."

11   Humanities programs overall experienced significant increases in the number of majors through 2012, when they began to decrease. It is difficult to say with certainty why the numbers have begun to decrease. The period coincides with a time of decreased funding for many humanities programs; one possibility is that the reduced support is a cause, rather than an effect, of decreased enrollments. For data, see Humanities Indicators, "Undergraduate and Graduate Education," especially charts indII-1a ("Bachelor's Degree Completions") and indII-1aa ("Bachelor's Degrees in the Humanities as a Percentage of All Bachelor's Degrees"). For analysis, see Hayot, "The Sky Is Falling," and Schmidt, "The Humanities Are in Crisis."

12   For a comprehensive plan for creating a sustainable teaching force, including conversion of some adjunct roles to full-time positions, see Bérubé and Ruth, *The Humanities, Higher Education, and Academic Freedom*.

13   Figlio, Schapiro, and Soter, "Are Tenure Track Professors Better Teachers?"

14   According to data from the Adjunct Project, the median per-course compensation at Northwestern is $5,000, compared to $2,700 across Illinois and $3,000 at four-year private not-for-profit institutions nationwide.

15   Johnson, "Glut of Postdoc Researchers Stirs a Quiet Crisis in Science."

16   Iasevoli, "A Glut of Ph.D.s Means Long Odds of Getting Jobs."

17   Nuffield Council on Bioethics, *The Culture of Scientific Research in the UK*, 31.

18   National Academy of Sciences, National Academy of Engineering, and the Institute of Medicine, *The Postdoctoral Experience Revisited*, 67–78.

19   The AAUP places the number around 70 percent, while the New Faculty Majority calculates it to be over 75 percent. Again, much depends on the ways the positions are counted.

20   Thanks to a new contract negotiated by PSC-CUNY, the union serving CUNY faculty, graduate students, and administrative staff, this was reduced to a 4–4 load in stages beginning in fall 2018 (Bowen, "Courseload Reduction").

21   According to the 2004 National Study of Postsecondary Faculty (NSOPF), the average number of classroom hours for faculty members teaching in public institutions offering associate's degrees was 18.1 hours per week, or approximately six courses per semester—far more than the average 9.4 hours/week (three courses/semester) of four-year institutions (NSOPF, table 21). The NSOPF provided the most robust data on matters related to faculty members and their work. However, the study was discontinued due to a lack of funding, and the most recent data, published in 2004, is more than a decade old. For more background on NSOPF, see the 2012 report by the Coalition on the Academic Workforce, "A Portrait of Part-Time Faculty Members." As that report notes, "The Department of Education provides some basic demographic data through the Integrated Postsecondary Education Data System (IPEDS) and previously collected more detailed information through the National Study of Postsecondary Faculty. After 2003, however, funding for the NSOPF ceased, and the department has not created an alternative instrument to gather information about the characteristics, work patterns, and working conditions of higher education's faculty workforce. As a result, the large and growing majority employed in contingent positions is rendered largely invisible, both as individuals on the campuses where they work and collectively in the ongoing policy discussions of higher education" (1).

22   Ziker, "How Professors Use Their Time."

23   Institute of Education Sciences, "IPEDS Data Center." For data analysis, see Laurence, "Our PhD Employment Problem, Part 2."

24   Coalition on the Academic Workforce, "A Portrait of Part-Time Faculty Members," table 9.

25   I discussed this topic in my remarks at the 2014 MLA Convention as part of a session titled "Who Benefits? Competing Agendas and Ethics in Graduate Education." While graduate program enrollment rates were not the primary focus of the session, the discussion largely circled around the question of whether graduate programs should shrink in order to improve the career prospects of PhDs. The topic elicited many strong opinions; in fact, a follow-up article in *Inside Higher Ed* called the topic "The Third Rail" (Jaschik, "Speakers at MLA Generally Are Skeptical of Idea of Shrinking Ph.D. Programs").

26   Stommel, "Why I Don't Grade."

27   Rumsey, "Creating Value and Impact in the Digital Age through Translational Humanities."

28   Machado, "O Adjunct! My Adjunct!"; Fredrickson, "There Is No Excuse for How

Universities Treat Adjuncts"; Hall, "I Am an Adjunct Professor Who Teaches Five Classes"; Anderson, "What Really Happened to Margaret Mary Vojtko, the Duquesne Adjunct Whose Death Became a Rallying Cry?"

29 For more on this, see Gordon and Hedlund, "Accounting for the Rise in College Tuition"; and Lucca, Nadauld, and Shen, "Credit Supply and the Rise in College Tuition."

30 For more detail on spending patterns in colleges and universities over time, see the Delta Cost Project. In particular, see Desrochers and Kirshstein, "Labor Intensive or Labor Expensive?"

31 My deep thanks to Bethany Nowviskie and Abby Smith Rumsey for making this possible.

32 At the time of writing, a new contract that would increase the minimum rate for adjunct faculty was pending member ratification. If the contract is ratified, the new rate for a three-credit course would increase to $5,500 by 2022.

33 Moten and Harney, "The University and the Undercommons," 102.

34 For more, see Bérubé and Ruth, *The Humanities, Higher Education, and Academic Freedom*, chapter 3.

35 MacNell, Driscoll, and Hunt, "What's in a Name"; Schmidt, "Gendered Language in Teaching Evaluations."

Chapter 2: Inclusive Systems, Vibrant Scholarship

1 hooks, *Teaching to Transgress*, 140.

2 Ashkenas, Park, and Pearce, "Even with Affirmative Action, Blacks and Hispanics Are More Underrepresented at Top Colleges Than 35 Years Ago."

3 Savonick and Davidson, "Gender Bias in Academe."

4 Matthew, *Written/Unwritten*.

5 Muhs, Niemann, González, and Harris, *Presumed Incompetent*.

6 Ahmed, *On Being Included*.

7 Bureau of Labor Statistics, "Earnings and Unemployment Rates by Educational Attainment," October 24, 2017.

8 Survey of Earned Doctorates, "Doctorate Recipients from U.S. Universities: 2016," fig. 3A.

9 I suspect this is also true for people who identify with other groups that are underrepresented or marginalized as well, such as people with disabilities or those who identify as LGBTQ+, but reliable data is not available.

10 National Center for Education Statistics, "The Condition of Education: Characteristics of Postsecondary Faculty," fig. 2. Racial and ethnic categories in the survey include White, Black, Hispanic, Asian/Pacific Islander, American Indian/Alaska Native, and two or more races/ethnicities.

11 For analysis of this point, see, for instance, Haley, Jaeger, and Levin, "The Influence of Cultural Social Identity on Graduate Student Career Choice."

12 Gibbs, Basson, Xierali, and Broniatowski, "Decoupling of the Minority PhD Talent Pool and Assistant Professor Hiring in Medical School Basic Science Departments in the US."

13 National Center for Education Statistics, "Fast Facts: Race/Ethnicity of College Faculty."

14 Humanities Indicators, "Trends in the Demographics of Humanities Faculty: Key Findings from the 2012–13 Humanities Departmental Survey," fig. HDS2-Fac5.

15 Humanities Indicators, "Earnings of Humanities Ph.D.'s," fig. III-8b.

16 US Department of Labor, Women's Bureau, "Number of Full-Time Workers and Median Earnings of Full-Time Workers by Occupation."

17 See, for instance, Miller, "A Child Helps Your Career, if You're a Man" (citing data from Michelle Budig), and Mason, Wolfinger, and Goulden, *Do Babies Matter?*.

18 In "Demarginalizing the Intersection of Race and Sex," Kimberlé Crenshaw coined the now-familiar (though often misused) term "intersectionality" to describe the ways in which Black women face particularly entrenched bias and subjugation due to the intersection of their gender and racial identity. The term has come to be used more broadly in reference to many different elements of identity, such as race, gender, immigration status, or socioeconomic status.

19 Matthew, *Written/Unwritten*, xiv–xv.

20 Matthew, *Written/Unwritten*, 5.

21 McCoy and Winkle-Wagner, "Bridging the Divide," 436. For more on this topic, see Stephens, Hamedani, and Destin, "Closing the Social-Class Achievement Gap," and Lareau, "Cultural Knowledge and Social Inequality."

22 Humanities Indicators, table II-12b. In this dataset, students are considered members of underrepresented groups if they are US citizens or permanent residents and self-identify as African American, Hispanic, or American Indian/ Alaska Native.

23 Posselt and Garces, "Expanding the Racial Diversity and Equity Agenda to Graduate Education," 444.

24 Posselt, *Inside Graduate Admissions*, 486. Based on a reading of Pierre Bourdieu, *Homo Academicus*.

25 Guinier, *The Tyranny of the Meritocracy*.

26 Ahmed, *On Being Included*.

27 For more, see Lipsitz, *The Possessive Investment in Whiteness*.

28 Haley, Jaeger, and Levin, "The Influence of Cultural Social Identity on Graduate Student Career Choice," 104.

29 Posselt, *Inside Graduate Admissions*; see especially chapter 2.

30 Posselt, *Inside Graduate Admissions*, 73.

31 Chuh, "On (Not) Mentoring."

32 Posselt, *Inside Graduate Admissions*, 57–58.

33 See, for instance, Posselt and Garces, "Expanding the Racial Diversity and Equity Agenda to Graduate Education," 444–45: "Due to the increasingly tight correspondence between credentials and career opportunities in many professions, racial stratification in graduate education shapes racial stratification in the labor market. . . . Attending to racial disparities also improves the educational experi-

ences of all students, helps students of color who enroll to persist through graduation, and expands the pipeline of faculty of color in graduate fields of study."

34 Sowell, Allum, and Okahana, "Doctoral Initiative on Minority Attrition and Completion."

35 Jerkins, "For a Writer of Color, Is Twitter More Valuable Than an MFA?"

36 Morrison, "Tacit Knowledge and Graduate Education."

37 Polk, "Making the Implicit Explicit—#tacitPhD."

38 See, for example, Zevallos, "Protecting Activist Academics against Public Harassment," and Cottom, "Everything but the Burden."

39 Muhs, Niemann, González, and Harris, *Presumed Incompetent*, 4.

Chapter 3: Expanding Definitions of Scholarly Success

1 Institute of Education Sciences, "IPEDS Data Center," accessed June 20, 2018, http://nces.ed.gov/ipeds/datacenter/. Data based on 2015–2016 enrollments.

2 State Higher Education Executive Officers, "SHEF—State Higher Education Finance FY14."

3 Posselt, *Inside Graduate Admissions*, 105.

4 Thanks to Jade Davis for suggesting this added valence to the image of the university as tower.

5 Abby Kluchin, Ajay Chaudhary, and Suzanne Schneider, telephone conversation with the author, January 12, 2017.

6 Matthew, *Written/Unwritten*, 229.

7 Visconti, "Infinite *Ulysses*."

8 "What Is a Dissertation?," HASTAC.

9 Dalgleish and Powell, "Beyond the Dissertation as Proto-Monograph: Examples and Reflections" and "Beyond the Dissertation as Proto-Monograph: Process and Experimentation."

10 Bissell et al., "The Knotted Line."

11 Ahmed et al., "Torn Apart / Separados." For a full list of credits, see http://xpmethod.plaintext.in/torn-apart/credits.html.

12 Davidson et al., "What Is a Dissertation?"

13 Bradley, "PhD Thesis Opens New Doors for Deaf Scholars."

14 Sousanis, *Unflattening*.

15 Presner, "Welcome to the Twenty-Year Dissertation."

16 Dalgleish and Powell, "Beyond the Dissertation as Proto-Monograph: Examples and Reflections" and "Beyond the Dissertation as Proto-Monograph: Process and Experimentation."

17 Fitzpatrick, *Generous Thinking*. Open peer review took place online at "Generous Thinking: The University and the Public Good" (*Humanities Commons*, 2018), https://generousthinking.hcommons.org/.

18 Fitzpatrick, *Planned Obsolescence*.

19 I contributed to the development of the Praxis Network as part of my role with SCI.

20 These include the Praxis Program at the University of Virginia; the Cultural

Heritage Informatics Initiative at Michigan State University; the Digital Fellows program at the Graduate Center, CUNY; the PhD Lab at Duke University; the joint MA/MSc program in Digital Humanities at University College London; the Digital Humanities program at the University of Canterbury in New Zealand (graduate and undergraduate); the Interactive Arts and Sciences Program at Brock University in Canada (undergraduate); and the Mellon Scholars program at Hope College (undergraduate).

21 Two examples include Prism, a collaborative annotation tool (http://prism.scholarslab.org), and Ivanhoe, a textual roleplaying game (http://ivanhoe.scholarslab .org).

22 At the time of writing, examples of past fellows' postgraduate employment include digital scholarship coordinator, Humanities and History Division, Columbia University Libraries (Alex Gil); digital arts and humanities specialist, Tufts University (Annie Swafford); head of graduate programs, Scholars' Lab, University of Virginia (Brandon Walsh); assistant professor of social and cultural analysis, New York University (Cecilia Márquez); marketing specialist, Milyli (an e-discovery software company) (Brooke Lestock); CLIR postdoctoral fellow, Duke University Library and Wired! Lab (Ed Triplett).

23 Brandon Walsh, email exchange with the author, January 29, 2019.

Chapter 4: What Faculty and Advisors Can Do

1 Two very good resources for faculty members are "Promising Practices in Humanities PhD Professional Development" (Council of Graduate Schools), and the Modern Language Association's "Graduate Student Career Planning Guide," which carries the added benefit of helping to establish norms for professional pathways in language and literature fields.

2 Thanks to Maureen McCarthy, director of the Center for Research and Scholarship at Quinnipiac University, for highlighting the connotations of this phrasing.

3 For more on this, see Muhs et al., *Presumed Incompetent*.

4 One of the most concrete examples of how institutions can shift from employing a large number of adjuncts to a more stable employment model with robust shared governance comes from Bérubé and Ruth, *The Humanities, Higher Education, and Academic Freedom*. Their plan, which involves converting some adjunct lines to teaching-focused faculty lines, is perhaps the most practical and wide-reaching plan for structural reform that has been put forward to date, and, indeed, they have been able to instrumentalize it at their respective institutions. And yet there is a risk that this plan would effectively create a new two-tier system, with research-intensive positions held in higher esteem than teaching-intensive positions. I believe this in part simply because the academy as a whole does not seem to value teaching to the degree that it claims. Such a plan may cement an imbalance between research and teaching, such that teaching-focused roles will continue to be undervalued, despite the hard-won gains of shared governance, job security, and institutional support. Even if their plan is not per-

fect, however, it is a positive and concrete action that others can hopefully build upon. What is abundantly clear is that the current system must change.

5   For more on the challenges that students from families with low socioeconomic status face in navigating the hidden structures and politics of the university, see Terenzini, Cabrera, and Bernal, *Swimming against the Tide.*

6   Versatile PhD was acquired by the predictive analytics start-up PeplWorks in 2018. What PeplWorks will do with users' data is unclear. It is because of circumstances like this that I strongly prefer directing people to tools and platforms developed by educational and nonprofit organizations, rather than for-profit consultancies.

7   Wood, "What Doors Does a Ph.D. in History Open?"

8   American Historical Association, "Where Historians Work: An Interactive Database of History PhD Career Outcomes." For an overview of the project and preliminary analysis, see Swafford and Ruediger, "Every Historian Counts."

9   However, the data that for-profit institutions share may not be trustworthy; for much more on this topic, see Cottom, *Lower Ed.*

10   Rogers, "Humanities Unbound."

11   Rogers, "Humanities Unbound."

12   Nowviskie, "It Starts on Day One." Emphasis in the original.

13   Nerad and Cerny, "From Rumors to Facts." Already in 1999, the authors remarked that "for over 20 years the crisis in the academic job market for humanities PhDs has been lamented."

14   Woodrow Wilson National Fellowship Foundation, "The Responsive PhD: Innovations in U.S. Doctoral Education."

15   For an excellent overview of like-minded efforts, see McCarthy, "Summary of Prior Work in Humanities PhD Professional Development."

16   "UVic Co-Op Program and Career Services—University of Victoria," UVic.ca, accessed August 1, 2018, https://www.uvic.ca/coopandcareer.

17   "Cooperative Education in the Liberal Arts," College of Social Sciences and Humanities, Northeastern University, accessed August 1, 2018, https://cssh.northeastern.edu/experiential-learning-2/cooperative-education.

18   Sharpe, "Passion for Travel Brings a Humanities Grad Full Circle."

19   For these and other stories, see "Co-Op Student Experiences—University of Victoria," UVic.ca, accessed January 15, 2017, http://www.uvic.ca/coopandcareer/co-op/experiences/stories/index-old-filter.php.

20   "Simpson Center for the Humanities," Simpson Center for the Humanities, accessed June 17, 2013, http://depts.washington.edu/uwch/.

21   Rumsey, "Rethinking Humanities Graduate Education, March 2013," and "Rethinking Humanities Graduate Education, October 2012."

22   Pannapacker, "Cultivating Partnerships in the Digital Humanities."

23   Stanford University, "Alt Ac Speaker Series: Alternative Academic Career Paths for PhDs," 2013, http://vpge.stanford.edu/students/altacseries.html.

24   Pannapacker, "Just Look at the Data, if You Can Find Any."

25   For instance, see Patton, "Where Did Your Graduate Students End Up?"

1   Sarah Werner, email exchange with the author, February 19, 2013.

2   While the three categories typically evaluated for the tenure and promotion of faculty members are research, teaching, and service, service is nearly always undervalued. This is especially true in highly intensive research institutions, but it also tends to be true in teaching-focused colleges. Even if service is considered important, it is much more difficult to document and quantify for a tenure file, and therefore is often invisible. When thinking about career pathways, students may be better served by reframing work that falls under the rubric of "service" as "impact" or "institutional leadership," both of which give a clearer sense of the importance of this undervalued part of their work. This is why I choose to focus on "impact" as a core value.

3   While this kind of database or listing is rare to find for a program or university, third-party organizations, most notably Versatile PhD (established in 1999, but acquired by the predictive analytics start-up PeplWorks in 2018), have stepped in to fill the gap by collecting relevant job ads, fostering an online community, and facilitating in-person meet-ups. The Council of Graduate Schools is currently compiling this information for the 66+ programs participating in its PhD Career Pathways program as well.

4   For more details, visit each program's website: Digital Humanities Summer Institutes, http://dhsi.org; Humanities Intensive Learning and Teaching, http://dhtraining.org/hilt/; and the Digital Pedagogy Lab, http://www.digitalpedagogylab.com/.

5   Louis Pitschmann, email exchange with the author, January 30, 2013.

6   For concrete exercises and examples, consider materials from graduate career centers, such as the Career Planning Guide produced by the Graduate Center's Office of Career Planning and Professional Development. Some examples of career-related books that target people with PhDs include Basalla and Debelius, *So What Are You Going to Do with That?*; Chin, *PhD [Alternative] Career Clinic*; Feibelman, *A PhD Is Not Enough!*; Figler, *Complete Job-Search Handbook*; Fruscione and Baker, *Succeeding Outside the Academy*; Kelsky, *The Professor Is In*; and Sinche, *Next Generation PhD*.

7   For a list of contributors, see https://www.imaginephd.com/creators.

8   Modern Language Association, "Graduate Student Career Planning Guide." The Connected Academics program and the development of this guide were overseen by Stacy Hartman in her capacity as project manager.

9   Lamott, *Bird by Bird*, 21–27.

10 Bill S.2119.

11 Cain and Pelisson, "9 Places in the US Where Job Candidates May Never Have to Answer the Dreaded Salary Question Again."

12 However, whether all employees can and do take advantage of this time is another question. See Mims, "Google's '20 Percent Time,' Which Brought You Gmail and AdSense, Is Now as Good as Dead."

13 Waldman and Cauterucci, "Negotiating While Female."

14 Amanda Visconti, email exchange with the author, February 9, 2019.

Conclusion: Building a University Worth Fighting For

1 See Albritton, "Educating Our Own: The Historical Legacy of HBCUs and Their Relevance for Educating a New Generation of Leaders." I am indebted to Jade Davis, director of digital project management at Columbia University Libraries, for encouraging me to pursue this line of thinking.

"About This Report | Science and Engineering Doctorates—NCSES | US National Science Foundation—Nsf.Gov." Accessed May 11, 2018. https://www.nsf.gov/statistics /2018/nsf18304/report/about-this-report.cfm.

"Adjunct Project." *Chronicle of Higher Education*, 2012. http://adjunct.chronicle.com/.

Ahmed, Manan, Maira E. Álvarez, Sylvia A. Fernández, Alex Gil, Merisa Martinez, Moacir P. de Sá Pereira, Roopika Risam, and Linda Rodriguez. "Torn Apart / Separados," 2018. http://xpmethod.plaintext.in/torn-apart/.

Ahmed, Sara. *On Being Included: Racism and Diversity in Institutional Life*. Durham, NC: Duke University Press, 2012.

Albritton, Travis J. "Educating Our Own: The Historical Legacy of HBCUs and Their Relevance for Educating a New Generation of Leaders." *Urban Review* 44, no. 3 (September 1, 2012): 311–31. https://doi.org/10.1007/s11256-012-0202-9.

Anderson, L. V. "What Really Happened to Margaret Mary Vojtko, the Duquesne Adjunct Whose Death Became a Rallying Cry?" *Slate*, November 17, 2013. http:// www.slate.com/articles/news_and_politics/education/2013/11/death_of _duquesne_adjunct_margaret_mary_vojtko_what_really_happened_to_her .html.

"A Portrait of Part-Time Faculty Members." Coalition on the Academic Workforce, June 2012. http://www.academicworkforce.org/CAW_portrait_2012.pdf.

Ashkenas, Jeremy, Haeyoun Park, and Adam Pearce. "Even with Affirmative Action, Blacks and Hispanics Are More Underrepresented at Top Colleges Than 35 Years Ago." *New York Times*, August 24, 2017, sec. U.S. https://www.nytimes.com/inter active/2017/08/24/us/affirmative-action.html.

"Background Facts on Contingent Faculty." American Association of University Professors. Accessed December 30, 2015. http://www.aaup.org/issues/contingency /background-facts.

Basalla, Susan, and Maggie Debelius. *So What Are You Going to Do with That? A Guide for M.A.'s and Ph.D.'s Seeking Careers Outside the Academy*. New York: Farrar, Straus and Giroux, 2001.

Berens, Kathi Inman. "Digital Humanities 2013: My Talk." July 9, 2013. http:// kathiiberens.com/2013/07/19/dh-2013/.

Bérubé, Michael. "Humanities Unraveled." *Chronicle of Higher Education*, February 18, 2013. http://www.chronicle.com/article/Humanities-Unraveled/137291/.

Bérubé, Michael. "Presidential Address 2013—How We Got Here." PMLA 128, no. 3 (May 1, 2013): 530–41. https://doi.org/10.1632/pmla.2013.128.3.530.

Bérubé, Michael, and Jennifer Ruth. *The Humanities, Higher Education, and Academic Freedom: Three Necessary Arguments*. New York: Palgrave Macmillan, 2015.

"Bill S.2119." Accessed October 28, 2016. https://malegislature.gov/Bills/189/Senate/S2119.

Bissell, Evan, Erik Loyer, Tanya Orellana, Lisa Nowlain, and Josh Begley. "The Knotted Line." Accessed October 21, 2015. http://knottedline.com/.

"Board: Student Assistants Covered by the NLRA." National Labor Relations Board. Accessed September 2, 2016. https://www.nlrb.gov/news-outreach/news-story/board-student-assistants-covered-nlra-0.

Bodenner, Chris. "Why Would a Poor Kid Want to Work in Academia?" *Atlantic*, November 28, 2016. https://www.theatlantic.com/notes/2016/11/why-would-a-poor-kid-want-to-work-in-academia/508874/.

Bourdieu, Pierre. *Homo Academicus*. Stanford, CA: Stanford University Press, 1988.

Bousquet, Marc. *How the University Works: Higher Education and the Low-Wage Nation*. New York: New York University Press, 2008.

Bowen, Barbara. "Courseload Reduction." PSC CUNY, May 9, 2018. http://www.psc-cuny.org/clarion/may-2018/courseload-reduction.

Bradley, Zack. "PhD Thesis Opens New Doors for Deaf Scholars." University Affairs. Accessed November 17, 2015. http://www.universityaffairs.ca/news/news-article/phd-thesis-opens-new-doors-for-deaf-scholars/.

Cain, Áine, and Anaele Pelisson. "9 Places in the US Where Job Candidates May Never Have to Answer the Dreaded Salary Question Again." Business Insider, October 2017. http://www.businessinsider.com/places-where-salary-question-banned-us-2017-10.

"Career Planning Guide." Office of Career Planning and Professional Development, Graduate Center, City University of New York, 2017. https://careerplan.commons.gc.cuny.edu/resources/guide.

Cassuto, Leonard. *The Graduate School Mess: What Caused It and How We Can Fix It*. Cambridge, MA: Harvard University Press, 2015.

"CGS Announces Multi-University Project to Understand Career Pathways of STEM PhD Students and Alumni." Council of Graduate Schools, March 20, 2017. http://cgsnet.org/cgs-announces-multi-university-project-understand-career-pathways-stem-phd-students-and-alumni.

Chin, Jane Y. *PhD [Alternative] Career Clinic*. Los Angeles: 9Pillars, 2011.

Chuh, Kandice. "On (Not) Mentoring." *Social Text*, January 13, 2013. http://socialtextjournal.org/periscope_article/on-not-mentoring/.

"The Condition of Education: Characteristics of Postsecondary Faculty." National Center for Education Statistics, May 2018. https://nces.ed.gov/programs/coe/indicator_csc.asp.

Cottom, Tressie McMillan. "Everything but the Burden: Publics, Public Scholarship, and Institutions." *Tressiemc* (blog), May 12, 2015. https://tressiemc.com/uncategorized/everything-but-the-burden-publics-public-scholarship-and-institutions/.

Cottom, Tressie McMillan. *Lower Ed: The Troubling Rise of For-Profit Colleges in the New Economy*. New York: New Press, 2017.

Crenshaw, Kimberlé. "Demarginalizing the Intersection of Race and Sex: A Black

Feminist Critique of Antiracist Doctrine." *University of Chicago Legal Forum*, no. 1, article 8 (1989): 139–67. https://chicagounbound.uchicago.edu/cgi/viewcontent .cgi?article=1052&context=uclf.

"The Culture of Scientific Research in the UK." Nuffield Council on Bioethics, December 2014. http://nuffieldbioethics.org/wp-content/uploads/Nuffield_research _culture_full_report_web.pdf.

"CUNY Adjunct Project." Accessed July 23, 2018. https://cunyadjunctproject.org/.

Dalgleish, Melissa, and Daniel Powell, eds. "Beyond the Dissertation as Proto-Monograph: Examples and Reflections." #alt-academy: Alternative Academic Careers. Accessed July 6, 2018. http://mediacommons.futureofthebook.org/alt-ac /cluster/beyond-dissertation-1.

Dalgleish, Melissa, and Daniel Powell, eds. "Beyond the Dissertation as Proto-Monograph: Process and Experimentation." #alt-academy: Alternative Academic Careers. Accessed July 6, 2018. http://mediacommons.futureofthebook.org/alt-ac /cluster/beyond-dissertation-2.

Davidson, Cathy N., Jade E. Davis, Gregory T. Donovan, Amanda Licastro, and Nick Sousanis. "What Is a Dissertation? New Models, Methods, Media." #alt -academy: Alternative Academic Careers, December 30, 2014. http://media commons.futureofthebook.org/alt-ac/pieces/what-dissertation-new-models -methods-media.

Desrochers, Donna M., and Rita Kirshstein. "Labor Intensive or Labor Expensive? Changing Staffing and Compensation Patterns in Higher Education." Issue Brief. Delta Cost Project at American Institutes for Research, February 2014. https:// www.deltacostproject.org/product-types/issue-briefs.

"Doctorate Recipients from U.S. Universities 2016." Survey of Earned Doctorates. Arlington, VA: National Science Foundation, National Center for Science and Engineering Statistics, 2016. https://www.nsf.gov/statistics/2018/nsf18304/.

"Earnings and Unemployment Rates by Educational Attainment." Bureau of Labor Statistics, October 24, 2017. http://www.bls.gov/emp/ep_chart_001.htm.

"Earnings of Humanities Ph.D.'s." Humanities Indicators, June 2018. https://www .humanitiesindicators.org/content/indicatordoc.aspx?i=70.

"Fast Facts: Race/Ethnicity of College Faculty." National Center for Education Statistics, 2013. https://nces.ed.gov/fastfacts/display.asp?id=61.

Feibelman, Peter J. *A PhD Is Not Enough! A Guide to Survival in Science*. Rev. ed. New York: Basic Books, 2011.

Figler, Howard E. *Complete Job-Search Handbook: Everything You Need to Know to Get the Job You Really Want*. 3rd ed. New York: Holt Paperbacks, 1999.

Figlio, David N., Morton O. Schapiro, and Kevin B. Soter. "Are Tenure Track Professors Better Teachers?" Working Paper. National Bureau of Economic Research, September 2013. http://www.nber.org/papers/w19406.

Fitzpatrick, Kathleen. "Generous Thinking: The University and the Public Good." Humanities Commons, 2018. https://generousthinking.hcommons.org/.

Fitzpatrick, Kathleen. *Generous Thinking: The University and the Public Good*. Baltimore: Johns Hopkins University Press, 2019.

Fitzpatrick, Kathleen. *Planned Obsolescence: Publishing, Technology, and the Future of the Academy.* New York: New York University Press, 2011.

Flaherty, Colleen. "U Wisconsin-Stevens Point to Eliminate 13 Majors." *Inside Higher Ed*, March 6, 2018. https://www.insidehighered.com/quicktakes/2018/03/06/u-wisconsin-stevens-point-eliminate-13-majors.

Fredrickson, Caroline. "There Is No Excuse for How Universities Treat Adjuncts." *Atlantic*, September 15, 2015. http://www.theatlantic.com/business/archive/2015/09/higher-education-college-adjunct-professor-salary/404461/.

Fruscione, Joseph, and Kelly J. Baker, eds. *Succeeding outside the Academy: Career Paths beyond the Humanities, Social Sciences, and STEM.* Lawrence: University Press of Kansas, 2018.

Gibbs, Kenneth D., Jacob Basson, Imam M. Xierali, and David A. Broniatowski. "Research: Decoupling of the Minority PhD Talent Pool and Assistant Professor Hiring in Medical School Basic Science Departments in the US." *ELife* 5 (November 17, 2016): e21393. https://doi.org/10.7554/eLife.21393.

Gordon, Grey, and Aaron Hedlund. "Accounting for the Rise in College Tuition." *NBER Working Paper*, September 28, 2015.

"Graduate Student Career Planning Guide." Modern Language Association, May 2017. https://connect.mla.hcommons.org/doctoral-student-career-planning-faculty-toolkit/.

"Guidelines for Evaluating Work in Digital Humanities and Digital Media." Modern Language Association, January 2012. http://www.mla.org/guidelines_evaluation_digital.

Guinier, Lani. *The Tyranny of the Meritocracy: Democratizing Higher Education in America.* Boston: Beacon Press, 2015.

Gupta, Suman, Jernej Habjan, and Hrvoje Tutek. *Academic Labour, Unemployment and Global Higher Education: Neoliberal Policies of Funding and Management.* London: Palgrave Macmillan, 2016.

Haley, Karen J., Audrey J. Jaeger, and John S. Levin. "The Influence of Cultural Social Identity on Graduate Student Career Choice." *Journal of College Student Development* 55, no. 2 (2014): 101–19. https://doi.org/10.1353/csd.2014.0017.

Hall, Lee. "I Am an Adjunct Professor Who Teaches Five Classes: I Earn Less Than a Pet-Sitter." *Guardian*, June 22, 2015. https://www.theguardian.com/commentisfree/2015/jun/22/adjunct-professor-earn-less-than-pet-sitter.

Hayot, Eric. "The Sky Is Falling." *Profession*, May 21, 2018. https://profession.mla.hcommons.org/2018/05/21/the-sky-is-falling/.

"The Heart of the Matter." American Academy of Arts & Sciences, June 2013. http://humanitiescommission.org/.

"Here's the News: The Annual Report on the Economic Status of the Profession, 2012–13." American Association of University Professors, April 2013. http://www.aaup.org/report/heres-news-annual-report-economic-status-profession-2012-13.

"Higher Education at a Crossroads: The Annual Report on the Economic Status of the Profession, 2015–16." Academe, American Association of University

Professors, April 2016. https://www.aaup.org/report/higher-education-crossroads
-annual-report-economic-status-profession-2015-16.

Holling, Michelle, May Fu, and Roe Bubar. "Dis/Jointed Appointments: Solidarity
amidst Inequity, Tokenism, and Marginalization." In *Presumed Incompetent: The
Intersections of Race and Class for Women in Academia*, edited by Gabriella Gutiérrez
y Muhs, Yolanda Flores Niemann, Carmen G. Gonzalez, and Angela P. Harris,
250–65. Boulder, CO: Utah State University Press, 2012.

hooks, bell. *Teaching to Transgress: Education as the Practice of Freedom.* New York: Rout-
ledge, 1994.

"Hymn: A New Poem by Sherman Alexie." Early Bird Books, August 16, 2017. https://
earlybirdbooks.com/hymn-a-new-poem-by-sherman-alexie.

Iasevoli, Brenda. "A Glut Of Ph.D.s Means Long Odds of Getting Jobs." NPR.org,
February 27, 2015. http://www.npr.org/sections/ed/2015/02/27/388443923/a-glut-of
-ph-d-s-means-long-odds-of-getting-jobs.

"Imagine PhD." ImaginePhD, June 4, 2018. https://www.imaginephd.com/creators.

Institute of Education Sciences. "IPEDS Data Center." Accessed June 17, 2014. http://
nces.ed.gov/ipeds/datacenter/.

Jaschik, Scott. "Skepticism about Tenure, MOOCs, and the Presidency: A Survey of
Provosts." *Inside Higher Ed*, January 23, 2013. http://www.insidehighered.com/news
/survey/skepticism-about-tenure-moocs-and-presidency-survey-provosts.

Jaschik, Scott. "Speakers at MLA Generally Are Skeptical of Idea of Shrinking Ph.D.
Programs." *Inside Higher Ed*, January 13, 2014. https://www.insidehighered.co
/news/2014/01/13/speakers-mla-generally-are-skeptical-idea-shrinking-phd
-programs.

Jerkins, Morgan. "For a Writer of Color, Is Twitter More Valuable Than an MFA?"
Pacific Standard. Accessed October 9, 2017. https://psmag.com/social-justice
/writer-of-color-twitter-more-valuable-than-mfa.

Johnson, Carolyn Y. "Glut of Postdoc Researchers Stirs a Quiet Crisis in Science."
Boston Globe, October 5, 2014, sec. Metro. https://www.bostonglobe.com/metro
/2014/10/04/glut-postdoc-researchers-stirs-quiet-crisis-science/HWxyErx9
RNIW17khvoMWTN/story.html.

June, Audrey Williams, and Jonah Newman. "Adjunct Project Reveals Wide Range in
Pay." *Chronicle of Higher Education*, January 4, 2013. http://chronicle.com/article
/Adjunct-Project-Shows-Wide/136439/.

Kelsky, Karen. *The Professor Is In: The Essential Guide to Turning Your Ph.D. into a Job.*
New York: Three Rivers Press, 2015.

Lamott, Anne. *Bird by Bird: Some Instructions on Writing and Life.* New York: Anchor,
1995.

Lareau, Annette. "Cultural Knowledge and Social Inequality." *American Sociological
Review* 80, no. 1 (February 1, 2015): 1–27. https://doi.org/10.1177/0003122414565814.

Laurence, David. "Our PhD Employment Problem, Part 2." *The Trend* (blog), March 11,
2014. http://mlaresearch.commons.mla.org/2014/03/11/our-phd-employment
-problem-part-2/.

Laurence, David. "Where Are They Now? Occupations of 1996–2011 PhD Recipients in 2013." *The Trend* (blog), February 18, 2015. https://mlaresearch.commons .mla.org/2015/02/17/where-are-they-now-occupations-of-1996-2011-phd-recipients -in-2013-2/.

Lipsitz, George. *The Possessive Investment in Whiteness: How White People Profit from Identity Politics,* revised and expanded edition. Philadelphia: Temple University Press, 2006.

Lucca, David O., Taylor Nadauld, and Karen Shen. "Credit Supply and the Rise in College Tuition: Evidence from the Expansion in Federal Student Aid Programs." *Federal Reserve Bank of New York Staff Reports,* no. 733 (July 2015). https://www.new yorkfed.org/medialibrary/media/research/staff_reports/sr733.pdf.

Machado, Carmen Maria. "O Adjunct! My Adjunct!" *New Yorker,* March 25, 2015. http://www.newyorker.com/books/page-turner/o-adjunct-my-adjunct.

MacNell, Lillian, Adam Driscoll, and Andrea N. Hunt. "What's in a Name: Exposing Gender Bias in Student Ratings of Teaching." *Innovative Higher Education* 40, no. 4 (August 1, 2015): 291–303. https://doi.org/10.1007/s10755-014-9313-4.

Main, Joyce B., Sarah Prenovitz, and Ronald G. Ehrenberg. "In Pursuit of a Tenure-Track Faculty Position: Career Progression and Satisfaction of Humanities and Social Sciences Doctorates." Working Paper. Cornell Higher Education Research Institute, December 2017. https://www.ilr.cornell.edu/sites/ilr.cornell.edu/files /CHERI%20WP180.pdf.

Mason, Mary Ann, Nicholas H. Wolfinger, and Marc Goulden. *Do Babies Matter? Gender and Family in the Ivory Tower.* New Brunswick, NJ: Rutgers University Press, 2013.

Matthew, Patricia A. *Written/Unwritten: Diversity and the Hidden Truths of Tenure.* Chapel Hill: University of North Carolina Press, 2016.

McCarthy, Maureen Terese. "Promising Practices in Humanities PhD Professional Development: Lessons Learned from the 2016–2017 Next Generation Humanities PhD Consortium." Council of Graduate Schools, September 2017. https://cgsnet .org/promising-practices-humanities-phd-professional-development-lessons -learned-2016-2017-next.

McCarthy, Maureen Terese. "Summary of Prior Work in Humanities PhD Professional Development." Council of Graduate Schools, September 2017. https:// cgsnet.org/ckfinder/userfiles/files/NEH_NextGen_PriorWork.pdf.

McCarty, Willard. "Getting There from Here: Remembering the Future of Digital Humanities." Busa Award Lecture presented at the Digital Humanities 2013 conference, August 12, 2013. https://www.youtube.com/watch?v=nTHa1rDR68o.

McCoy, Dorian L., and Rachelle Winkle-Wagner. "Bridging the Divide: Developing a Scholarly Habitus for Aspiring Graduate Students through Summer Bridge Programs Participation." *Journal of College Student Development* 56, no. 5 (2015): 423–39. https://doi.org/10.1353/csd.2015.0054.

Miller, Claire Cain. "A Child Helps Your Career, if You're a Man." *New York Times,* September 6, 2014, sec. The Upshot. https://www.nytimes.com/2014/09/07 /upshot/a-child-helps-your-career-if-youre-a-man.html.

Mims, Christopher. "Google's '20% Time,' Which Brought You Gmail and AdSense,

Is Now as Good as Dead." *Quartz*, August 16, 2013. http://qz.com/115831
/googles-20-time-which-brought-you-gmail-and-adsense-is-now-as-good-as-dead/.
"MLA Recommendation on Minimum Per-Course Compensation for Part-Time Faculty Members." Modern Language Association, April 2015. https://www.mla.org
/Resources/Research/Surveys-Reports-and-Other-Documents/Staffing-Salaries
-and-Other-Professional-Issues/MLA-Recommendation-on-Minimum-Per-Course
-Compensation-for-Part-Time-Faculty-Members.
"Monuments and Memory Reading List." Google Doc. Accessed April 20, 2018.
https://docs.google.com/document/d/1ljtWytjwkUlOqF8JNIRWTqeeXBkSbo
WiYHVYHGgtcow/mobilebasic.
Morrison, Aimée. "Tacit Knowledge and Graduate Education." *Hook & Eye* (blog),
September 16, 2015. https://hookandeye.ca/2015/09/16/tacit-knowledge-and
-graduate-education/.
Morrison, Toni. "Making America White Again." *New Yorker*, November 14, 2016.
https://www.newyorker.com/magazine/2016/11/21/making-america-white-again.
Moten, Fred, and Stefano Harney. "The University and the Undercommons: Seven
Theses." *Social Text* 22, no. 2 (79) (June 1, 2004): 101–15. https://doi.org/10.1215
/01642472-22-2_79-101.
Muhs, Gabriella Gutiérrez y, Yolanda Flores Niemann, Carmen G. González, and Angela P. Harris, eds. *Presumed Incompetent: The Intersections of Race and Class for Women in Academia*. Boulder, CO: Utah State University Press, 2012.
National Academy of Sciences, National Academy of Engineering, and Institute of
Medicine. *The Postdoctoral Experience Revisited*. 2014. http://www.nap.edu/catalog
/18982/the-postdoctoral-experience-revisited.
"National Adjunct Walkout Day." Accessed July 23, 2018. http://nationaladjunct
.tumblr.com/.
National Center for Education Statistics. "Fast Facts: Race/Ethnicity of College Faculty." Accessed July 5, 2018. https://nces.ed.gov/fastfacts/display.asp?id=61.
National Center for Education Statistics. "National Study of Postsecondary Faculty."
Data Analysis System—NSOPF Tables. Accessed December 29, 2016. https://nces
.ed.gov/das/library/tables_listings/2006176.asp.
Nerad, Maresi, and Joseph Cerny. "From Rumors to Facts: Career Outcomes of English PhDs." *ADE Bulletin* 32, no. 7 (Fall 1999): 11.
"New Faculty Majority." New Faculty Majority. Accessed January 29, 2017. http://
www.newfacultymajority.info/.
Newfield, Christopher. *Unmaking the Public University: The Forty-Year Assault on the Middle Class*. Reprint ed. Cambridge, MA: Harvard University Press, 2011.
Nowviskie, Bethany. "#altac Origin Stories (with Tweets)." Storify, 2012. http://
storify.com/nowviskie/altac-origin-stories.
Nowviskie, Bethany. "Fight Club Soap." June 9, 2010. http://nowviskie.org/2010
/fight-club-soap/.
Nowviskie, Bethany. "It Starts on Day One." *Chronicle of Higher Education. ProfHacker*
(blog), January 12, 2012. http://chronicle.com/blogs/profhacker/it-starts-on-day
-one/37893.

"Number of Full-Time Workers and Median Earnings of Full-Time Workers by Occupation." US Department of Labor, Women's Bureau, Data and Statistics. Accessed
June 19, 2019. https://www.dol.gov/wb/stats/stats_data.htm.

"Occupations of Humanities PhDs, Chart III-7a." Humanities Indicators, 2015.
http://www.humanitiesIndicators.org/content/indicatorDoc.aspx?i=69.

O'Keefe, Ed. "Members of White House Presidential Arts Committee Resigning to
Protest Trump's Comments." *Washington Post*, August 18, 2017. https://www
.washingtonpost.com/news/powerpost/wp/2017/08/18/members-of-white-house
-presidential-arts-commission-resign-to-protest-trumps-comments/.

Pannapacker, William. "Cultivating Partnerships in the Digital Humanities."
Chronicle of Higher Education, May 13, 2013. http://chronicle.com/article
/Cultivating-Partnerships-in/139161/.

Pannapacker, William. "Just Look at the Data, if You Can Find Any." *Chronicle of
Higher Education*, June 17, 2013. http://chronicle.com/article/Just-Look-at-the
-Data-if-You/139795/.

Patton, Stacey. "Where Did Your Graduate Students End Up? LinkedIn Knows."
Chronicle of Higher Education, June 11, 2012. http://chronicle.com/article/Where
-Did-Your-Graduate/132197/.

"The Ph.D. Placement Project." *The Ph.D. Placement Project—The Chronicle of Higher
Education* (blog), 2013. http://chronicle.com/blogs/phd/.

Polk, Jennifer. "Making the Implicit Explicit—#tacitPhD." *Storify* (blog), September 17,
2015. https://storify.com/FromPhDtoLife/making-the-implicit-explicit-tacitphd.

Posselt, Julie R. *Inside Graduate Admissions: Merit, Diversity, and Faculty Gatekeeping.*
Cambridge, MA: Harvard University Press, 2016.

Posselt, Julie R., and Liliana M. Garces. "Expanding the Racial Diversity and Equity
Agenda to Graduate Education." *American Journal of Education* 120, no. 4 (2014):
443–49. https://doi.org/10.1086/676907.

Presner, Todd. "Welcome to the 20-Year Dissertation." *Chronicle of Higher Education*,
November 25, 2013. http://chronicle.com/article/Welcome-to-the-20-Year/143223/.

Reed, Shannon. "Classic College Movies Updated for the Adjunct Era." McSweeney's
Internet Tendency, August 19, 2016. https://www.mcsweeneys.net/articles
/classic-college-movies-updated-for-the-adjunct-era.

"Report of the Task Force on Doctoral Study in Modern Language and Literature."
2014. Modern Language Association. https://www.mla.org/Resources/Research
/Surveys-Reports-and-Other-Documents/Staffing-Salaries-and-Other-Professional
-Issues/Report-of-the-Task-Force-on-Doctoral-Study-in-Modern-Language-and
-Literature-2014.

"The Responsive PhD: Innovations in U.S. Doctoral Education." Woodrow Wilson
National Fellowship Foundation, September 2005. http://www.woodrow.org
/responsivephd/.

Rogers, Katina. "471. Who Benefits? Competing Agendas and Ethics in Graduate
Education." Chicago, 2014. https://apps.mla.org/conv_listings_detail?prog
_id=471&year=2014.

Rogers, Katina. "Humanities Unbound: Supporting Careers and Scholarship beyond

the Tenure Track." *DHQ: Digital Humanities Quarterly* 9, no. 1 (2015). http://www
.digitalhumanities.org/dhq/vol/9/1/000198/000198.html.

Rumsey, Abby Smith. "Creating Value and Impact in the Digital Age through Translational Humanities." *CLIR Ruminations*, April 25, 2013. http://www.clir.org/pubs
/ruminations/03smithrumsey/.

Rumsey, Abby Smith. "Rethinking Humanities Graduate Education." Walter Chapin
Simpson Center for the Humanities, University of Washington, March 11, 2013.
http://libra.virginia.edu/catalog/libra-oa:3266.

Savonick, Danica, and Cathy Davidson. "Gender Bias in Academe: An Annotated
Bibliography of Important Recent Studies." *Publications and Research*, February 27,
2017. https://academicworks.cuny.edu/qc_pubs/163.

Schmidt, Benjamin. "Gendered Language in Teaching Evaluations." February 2015.
http://benschmidt.org/profGender/#.

Schmidt, Benjamin. "The Humanities Are in Crisis." *Atlantic*, August 23, 2018.
https://www.theatlantic.com/education/archive/2018/08/the-humanities-face
-a-crisisof-confidence/567565/.

Seltzer, Beth, Roopika Risam, and Matt Applegate. "#MLA 2018: Digital Humanities
as Critical University Studies #s198." New York, 2018. https://mapplega.com
/2017/10/24/mla-2018-digital-humanities-as-critical-university-studies-s198/.

Sharpe, Tara. "Passion for Travel Brings a Humanities Grad Full Circle." The Ring,
November 4, 2015. http://ring.uvic.ca/news/passion-travel-brings-humanities
-grad-full-circle.

"SHEF—State Higher Education Finance FY14." State Higher Education Executive
Officers, April 12, 2015. http://www.sheeo.org/projects/shef-fy14.

Sinche, Melanie V. *Next Gen PhD: A Guide to Career Paths in Science.* Cambridge, MA:
Harvard University Press, 2016.

Smith, Sidonie. *Manifesto for the Humanities: Transforming Doctoral Education in Good
Enough Times.* Ann Arbor: University of Michigan Press, 2015.

Sousanis, Nick. *Unflattening.* Cambridge, MA: Harvard University Press, 2015.

Sowell, Robert, Jeff Allum, and Hironao Okahana. "Doctoral Initiative on Minority
Attrition and Completion." Council of Graduate Schools, 2015. https://cgsnet.org
/minority-attrition-and-completion-stem-doctoral-programs.

Stephens, Nicole M., MarYam G. Hamedani, and Mesmin Destin. "Closing the Social-
Class Achievement Gap: A Difference-Education Intervention Improves
First-Generation Students' Academic Performance and All Students' College
Transition." *Psychological Science* 25, no. 4 (April 1, 2014): 943–53. https://doi.org
/10.1177/0956797613518349.

Stommel, Jesse. "Why I Don't Grade." *Jesse Stommel* (blog), October 26, 2017. https://
www.jessestommel.com/why-i-dont-grade/.

Swafford, Emily, and Dylan Ruediger. "Every Historian Counts: A New AHA
Database Analyzes Careers for PhDs." *Perspectives on History, American Historical
Association* (blog), July 9, 2018. https://www.historians.org/publications-and
-directories/perspectives-on-history/september-2018/every-historian-counts-a-new
-aha-database-analyzes-careers-for-phds.

Swail, Watson Scott, Laura W. Perna, and Kenneth E. Redd. *Retaining Minority Students in Higher Education: A Framework for Success. ASHE-ERIC Higher Education Report. Jossey-Bass Higher and Adult Education Series.* San Francisco: Jossey-Bass, 2003. https://eric.ed.gov/?id=ED483024.

Terenzini, Patrick T., Alberto F. Cabrera, and Elena M. Bernal. *Swimming against the Tide: The Poor in American Higher Education. Research Report No. 2001-1.* College Entrance Examination Board, 2001. https://eric.ed.gov/?id=ED562879.

Tiede, Hans-Joerg. "Tenure and the University of Wisconsin System." *Academe*, American Association of University Professors, June 2016. https://www.aaup.org/article/tenure-and-university-wisconsin-system.

"Trends in the Demographics of Humanities Faculty: Key Findings from the 2012–13 Humanities Departmental Survey." Humanities Indicators, 2014. https://www.humanitiesindicators.org/content/indicatordoc.aspx?i=461#fig484.

"Undergraduate and Graduate Education." Humanities Indicators. Accessed June 20, 2018. https://www.humanitiesindicators.org/content/indicatorDoc.aspx?i=9.

Visconti, Amanda. "Infinite *Ulysses*." 2015. http://www.infiniteulysses.com/.

Waldman, Katy, and Christina Cauterucci. "Negotiating While Female: Sometimes It Does Hurt to Ask." *Slate*, March 17, 2014. http://www.slate.com/blogs/xx_factor/2014/03/17/should_women_negotiate_for_more_pay_a_female_academic_leans_in_and_allegedly.html.

Werner, Sarah. "Make Your Own Luck." *Wynken de Worde* (blog), January 7, 2013. http://sarahwerner.net/blog/2013/01/make-your-own-luck/.

"What Is a Dissertation? A Collection of Posts Related to #remixthediss." Humanities, Arts, Science, and Technology Alliance and Collaboratory (HASTAC). Accessed August 10, 2018. https://www.hastac.org/remixthediss.

"Where Historians Work: An Interactive Database of History PhD Career Outcomes." American Historical Association, 2018. https://www.historians.org/wherehistorianswork.

Wood, Maren. "What Doors Does a Ph.D. in History Open?" *Chronicle of Higher Education*, October 30, 2012. http://chronicle.com/article/What-Doors-Does-a-PhD-in/135448/.

Yong, Ed. "Science's Minority Talent Pool Is Growing—but Draining Away." *Atlantic*, November 22, 2016. http://www.theatlantic.com/science/archive/2016/11/the-minority-talent-pool-in-science-is-growing-and-draining-away/508481/.

Zevallos, Zuleyka. "Protecting Activist Academics against Public Harassment." *The Other Sociologist* (blog), July 6, 2017. https://othersociologist.com/2017/07/06/activist-academics-public-harassment/.

Ziker, John. "How Professors Use Their Time: Faculty Time Allocation." *Blue Review*, March 31, 2014. https://thebluereview.org/faculty-time-allocation/.

careers, faculty, 10, 12, 31, 45–46, 87, 138n11

careers, non-faculty: administrative, 31–32; and admissions processes, 53–54; alt-academic, viii, 13–14; importance of, 6, 34, 88; reasons for pursuing, 12, 14; types of, 10–11, 33; visibility of, 87–88

career searches: and the dissertation, 123–26; faculty *versus* non-faculty, 118; support materials, 117–18, 146n6; techniques, 118–19

career search tips: application materials, 119; attitude, 104–5, 114; credential biases, 114; for current students, 109–17; inspiration, finding, 111; interviews, 119–20; networking, 111–13; opportunities, taking, 110; pitching improvements, 111; professional organizations, 110–11; public-facing scholarship, 115; requirements, personal, 115–16; resources, using, 113; salary and negotiation, 120–23; skill building, 110; skill evaluation, 113–14; for students, prospective, 108–9; support, finding, 110; values, personal, 116

Chaudhary, Ajay, 60

Chuh, Kandice, 52, 54

City University of New York (CUNY): adjuncts at, 36; author's experiences at, xi–xii; enrollment, xi, 137n4; the Futures Initiative, xi, 84–85, 128; labor classification system, 36; mentorship programs, 54; Pipeline Program, 54; size of, xi; teaching loads at, 29, 140n20

Coalition on the Academic Workforce, 33

collaboration, 92–93

Commons Open Repository Exchange (CORE), 69

commons *versus* ivory towers, 60

community colleges, 29, 37, 87, 103, 116

community partnerships, 94–96, 98–99, 132–33

connection skills, 107

contingent labor, 6–7, 28, 35–36. *See also* adjunct teaching

co-op programs, 95

Council of Graduate Schools, 55, 86, 146n3

Davidson, Cathy, xi, 41

departments, conservatism of, 5–6

digital projects: accessibility of, 70; collaboration on, 70; dissertations, 64–68, 90, 123–26; "Infinite *Ulysses*," 63, 124; meaningful, 63–64; preservation of, 65–66; and success measures, 69–70; work-in-progress platforms, 68–69

dissertations: and accessibility, 65; and *#Alt-Academy* journal, 67–68; and career goals, 123–26; changing, effects of, 67; creative, 64–68, 90, 123–26; evaluating, 66, 125–26; functions of, 125; and institutional structures, 125; limitations on, 65–66; as professional development, 90; as project management, 126; translational work, 103–7, 124; valuation of, 68

diversity: barriers to, 5–6; enabling, 9–10; of faculty members, 44; institutional lack of, 39–44; and public engagement, 63; of undergraduates, 37

diversity initiatives, 40–41, 48–50

doctoral degree recipients: in academic positions, 6, 138n4; job satisfaction, 3; from marginalized groups, 47–48; networks of, 3–4; in non-academic positions, 3–5, 137n2; unemployment rates, 3–4, 6, 42, 137n2

doctoral degrees: as career credentials, xii; pursuing, reasons for, 8–10; translating for employers, 103–7

extracurricular programs, 74

Levin, John S., 50
Lilli Research Group, 86
love, rhetoric of, 21–23, 116

Machado, Carmen Maria, 35
marginalized groups: and advisors, 79; biases against, 41–42; doctoral degree recipients, 47–48; faculty career barriers, 51; hiring of, 56; mentorship of, 47; and public engagement, 62; salary negotiations, 121–22; service workloads, 47; undergraduate enrollment, 29, 49. *See also* structural inequality
Matthew, Patricia A., 41–42, 46, 62
McCoy, Dorian, 47
McDowell, Gary, 28
McKenna, Laura, 35
Mellon Foundation, 8, 95
mentorship: benefits of, 3; expanding, 83–85, 88; and identity, 47; importance of, 46–47; improvement recommendations, 78–80; invisibility of, 54; peer, 54–55, 84–85; professional valuation of, 54. *See also* advisor-student relationships
meritocracy, 48
methods courses, 91–94, 97–98, 134
minorities. *See* structural inequality
MLA Commons, 69
models, importance of, 134
Modern Language Association (MLA): adjunct compensation recommendations, 25; author's experiences at, x–xi; Doctoral Student Career Planning Guide, 117–18; employment research, 3–4; Task Force on Doctoral Education, 8
Morrison, Aimée, 55
Moten, Fred, 21–22, 37

National Endowment for the Humanities, 8
National Study of Postsecondary Faculty, 140n21

Nerad, Maresi, 93
Nowviskie, Bethany, viii, x, 92

parental involvement, 50
pipeline thinking, 43
Pitschmann, Louis, 114
Polk, Jennifer, 56
Posselt, Julie, 48, 51–52, 59, 142n33
postdoctoral positions, 28, 35
the Praxis Network, 72, 74, 143n19
Praxis Program, University of Virginia, 72–74, 143n20, 144nn21–22
Presner, Todd, 67
prestige: and career pathways, 87; damaging emphasis on, 88–89; *versus* impact, 69–72; as reform barrier, 129; of research, 78
professional associations, 97, 110
professional development: and academic ecosystems, 98; and the academic workforce, 23–24; career pathway visibility, 87–88, 99; curricula integration, 97; and dissertations, 90; early, 12, 133; feminist approaches to, 51; as lacking, 10, 20, 24, 79; and methods courses, 91–94, 97–98, 134; need for, 15; non-faculty careers, 11–12, 15; partnerships supporting, 94–96, 98–99; reform initiatives, 93–94; reform recommendations, 89–91, 96–100; and research, 79; resources, outside, 133–34; skills development, 92–93; skills framing, 91; in teaching, 37–38; training programs, 98
project management, 92–93
public engagement: benefits of, 9–10, 58–60, 130; Brooklyn Institute for Social Research, 60–61; desire for, 60; and inclusivity, 40, 71–72, 74–75; negative views of, 62; and reform, 135–36; and scholarly communication, 61; as success measure, 62–63, 74; and technology, 63–64; and tenure reviews,

62; valuations of, 59, 71; and works-in-progress, 68–69
the public good, 39–40, 58, 69
public scholarship, 58–63, 130
PublicsLab, 95
public university affordability, 58

Reed, Shannon, 25
reflection, importance of, 131–32
reform, graduate education, 2, 7–8
reform, institutional: adjunct teaching, 32–36; barriers to, 129; benefits of, 130; lack of, 128; sources of, 129; suggestions for, 131–36
research: and adjunct teaching, 28; emphasis on, 36–37, 78; goal of, 61; impact of, 2; and inclusivity, 40; prestige of, 78; and professional development, 79; translating for employers, 105–6; valuation of, 77–78, 103, 144n4
Responsive PhD program, 93
Rhody, Jason, viii
Risam, Roopika, 15
Rumsey, Abby Smith, 34
Ruth, Jennifer, 27–28, 144n4

Savonick, Danica, 41
Scalar, 64
Schapiro, Morton O., 27
scholarly communication: accessibility of, 65; changing norms, 126; digital projects, 63–64; innovation and equity, 61–62, 64; means of, 59–61; public, 61
Scholarly Communication Institute (SCI), x, xii. *See also* Humanities Unbound study
scholarship, expanding ideas of, 132
Seltzer, Beth, 15
service, 38, 47, 78, 146n2
shared governance, 27–30, 38
skills: applicability of, 15; building, 110; developing, 92–93; digital humanities, 13; essential *versus* ancillary, 14;

evaluating, 113–14; framing for employers, 91, 103; humanities students lacking, 93
Smith, Sidonie, 18
social media, 55–56
Soter, Kevin B., 27
Sousanis, Nick, 66
Stommel, Jesse, 33–34
structural inequality: accounts of, 41–42; admissions processes, 51–52; and advising, 79; combating, 135; contributing factors, 42–43; as dissuading students, 51; and first-generation students, 43, 47–48, 51; and gender, 45–46, 78; in higher faculty ranks, 44; in the humanities, 56; and love rhetoric, 23; and mentorship, 47; meritocracy, 48; minority representation, 41; push-pull dynamics, 45; retention problems, 44; salaries, 121–22; and service workloads, 47; success, hindering, 41; and success barriers, 43; tacit knowledge, 46–48, 55; and teaching devaluation, 77–78; tenure cases, 46; underrepresentation, faculty, 41; and values, 46
student services, 35
success, definitions of, 4, 41, 57, 81
success, expanding definitions of: benefits of, 40–41, 57, 60, 127; creative and digital projects, 63–64, 69–70; difficulties in, 71–72; and dissertations, 64–68; efforts toward, 8; and forms of scholarship, 69–70; and inclusivity, 41; institutional support, need for, 70; and public engagement, 62–63, 74; requirements for, 71; training programs, 73–74; and women, 46
success, measures of, 40, 69–72

tacit knowledge, 42–43, 46–48, 55, 80
teaching: at community colleges, 29, 37, 103, 116; at CUNY, 29, 140n20; graduate assistantships, 24; graduate

student, 30; importance of, 37; professional development in, 37–38; reinvesting in, 20, 36–38; *versus* research, 36–37; and structural inequality, 77–78; student evaluations, 38; translating for employers, 106–7; valuation of, 20, 77–78, 103, 144n4. *See also* adjunct teaching
teaching for food, 22
teaching loads, 25, 29, 78, 140nn20–21
tenure reviews, 46, 62, 146n2
tenure-track positions, 5–7, 26
Track, Report, Connect, Exchange program (TRaCE), 85
tuition, 35, 77, 94
tuition waivers, 30, 32
Twitter, viii, x, 55, 84, 112–13, 133

undergraduate students, 5, 26, 29, 139n11
underrepresented people. *See* marginalized groups; structural inequality
University of Victoria, 95

Versatile PhD, 85, 145n6, 146n3
Visconti, Amanda, 63, 124–25

Walsh, Brandon, 73
Werner, Sarah, xii, 102
whiteness, 42–43, 46, 48–49. *See also* structural inequality
Winkle-Wagner, Rachelle, 47
women: in administrative roles, 45; biases against, 41–42; challenges faced by, 51; of color, 46, 56; compensation, 45; higher faculty ranks, 44; hiring of, 56; negotiating job offers, 121–22; non-tenure-track, 45; service workloads, 47; and social media, 56. *See also* structural inequality
Woodward, Kathleen, 98
workforce casualization, 20

Ziker, John, 31

Students who
don't conform

help
guidance

data
info

Skills
in
Learning

Analyzing
a
Problem

Steps to
Finding
answer

via Research

Admission

Translate
information